# THE
# NEW YORKER
## BOOK OF TECHNOLOGY CARTOONS

BLOOMBERG PRESS

PRINCETON

# THE
# NEW YORKER
## BOOK OF
# TECHNOLOGY CARTOONS

EDITED AND WITH AN INTRODUCTION BY ROBERT MANKOFF
IN ASSOCIATION WITH CARTOONBANK.COM

PUBLISHED BY BLOOMBERG PRESS

To purchase framed prints of cartoons or to license cartoons for use in periodicals,
Web sites, or other media, please contact CARTOONBANK.COM, a New Yorker
Magazine company, at 145 Palisade Street, Suite 373, Dobbs Ferry, NY 10522,
Tel: 800-897-TOON, or (914) 478-5527, Fax: (914) 478-5604,
e-mail: toon@cartoonbank.com, Web: www.cartoonbank.com.

Books are available for bulk purchases at special discounts.
Special editions or book excerpts can also be created to specifications.
For information, please write: Special Markets Department, Bloomberg Press.

BLOOMBERG and BLOOMBERG PRESS are trademarks
and service marks of Bloomberg L.P. All rights reserved.

First edition published 2000

1  3  5  7  9  10  8  6  4  2

Library of Congress Cataloging-in-Publication Data


    The New Yorker book of technology cartoons / edited by and with an introduction
by Robert Mankoff.-- 1st ed.
        p.    cm.
    ISBN 1-57660-075-0 (alk. paper)
        1. Technology--Caricature and cartoons.  2. American wit and humor,
Pictorial.  I. Title: Book of technology cartoons. II. Mankoff, Robert. III. New Yorker
(New York, N.Y.: 1925)

    NC1428 .N47 2000
    741.5'973--dc21                                                    00-030390

**Book design by** LAURIE LOHNE / **Design It Communications**

# THE
# NEW YORKER
## BOOK OF TECHNOLOGY CARTOONS

BY ROBERT MANKOFF

# Welcome to the Introduction to 'The New Yorker *Book of Technology Cartoons*'

Please press any key to continue.

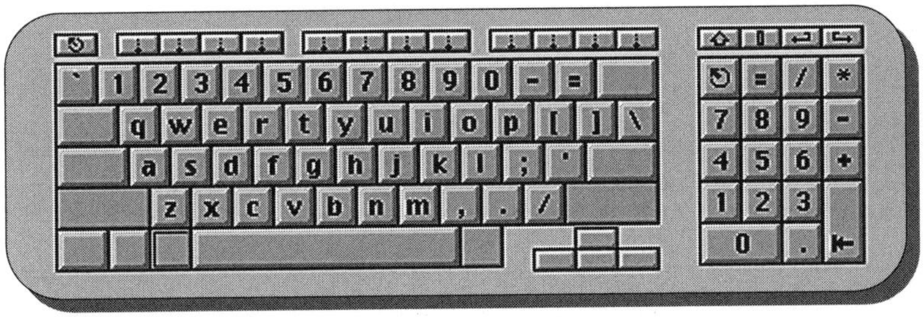

ALERT! Error Code—006#!%!!—No Key Pressed—Human Error—You. That's right, you. We know all about you. Our sophisticated tracking technology has been sending us your data ever since you purchased this book. And everything seemed OK until you refused to press that key. Now it appears you have an antitechnological tendency that has to be dealt with. My advice: get over it, move on—technology already has.

The essence of technology is change. In fact, the world of technology changes so fast that by the time you finish this introduction the first part of it will already be obsolete. Fortunately, an upgrade is already available and can be downloaded at www.bythetimeyoufinishthisintroductionthefirstpartofitwillbe-obsolete.com or at its mirror site: moc.etelosboeblliwtifotraptsrifehtnoitcudortni-sihthsinifuoyemitehtyb.www.

If downloading the upgrade fails, upgrading your download software may be required. However, if that exceeds the meager bandwidth of your wetware, versions of the introduction's upgrade are also available offline at fine NotDot-Com stores everywhere in CD, DVD, and the increasingly popular BVD formats (S, M, L, or XL).

As you may have guessed by now, I'm a technophile. Look, it could be worse. I could be a Francophile. Actually, it's more complicated than that; I have a love-hate relationship with technology—I love it when it works, and I hate it when it doesn't. But even when the technology works, I often find myself resenting it. Like when my communications center tells me I have no voice mail, no pager messages, no e-mail, and no friends. Or when my Global Positioning System, which is constantly tracking my exact spot on Earth to within fifty feet, suggests that really, I should get out more. Or when my computer cannot find a chess level low enough to play with me and recommends a "smart" appliance as a suitable opponent. (Or when the appliance wins.) At moments like these I find myself quickly changing from a mild-mannered technophile to a wild-mannered technopath.

But these technocidal impulses never hold sway for long. And before you can say "dot-com," I'm plunging ever deeper into a world where Murphy's Law combines with Moore's Law to insure that everything that can go wrong will go wrong, but at twice the rate that it did eighteen months ago. Example: I've got a new electronic organizer clipped right on the back of my cell phone. And the phone has been tweaked to function as a wireless modem for my laptop, which can now transfer e-mails back to my organizer, which, of course, causes it to run out of memory. Now, I could get more memory for the organizer, or I could wait for the next product cycle to spawn an updated version that could handle the increased message load. This new organizer would undoubtedly require me to replace all the other equipment in my high-tech scheme, but frankly, it's about time I got rid of all that old junk anyway.

The absurdity of all this is not lost on me. As soon as I put my e-check in the e-mail for the latest e-thing I'm thinking, "Egad! I've become desperately dependent on an army of devices that I don't need." It makes me wonder: if, as all the information-age pundits tell me, technology is my servant, how come I've become its slave?

I'd like to place the blame for all this on the new economy, the new media, the new paradigm, or that new e-thing I just bought, but the real culprit is just plain old me, as this fifteen-year-old, very autobiographical *New Yorker* cartoon of mine attests.

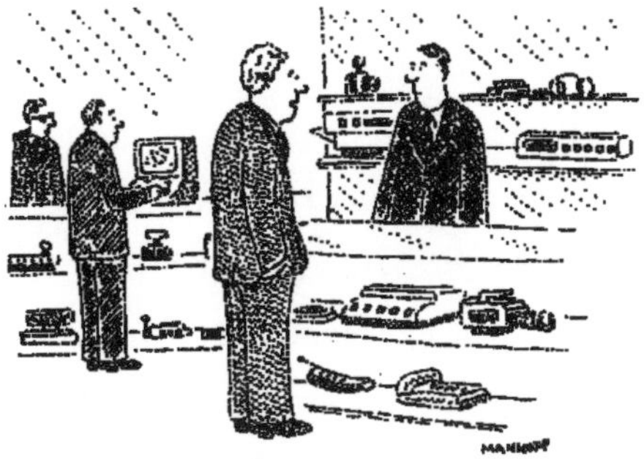

*"All my gadgets are old. I'd like some new gadgets."*

Basically, I never met a consumer technology I didn't like. You build it, and I'll buy it. Why? Well, if this pocket genome decoder of mine is correct, it's because I'm hardwired for it.

Other cartoonists are wired a bit differently. The ones in this book represent a continuum with me over at one end (some would say the deep end) while on the other end are guys like Charlie Barsotti and Jack Ziegler, who view any technology later than that of the technical pen with suspicion. Although they use computers and their ilk, their attitude, as expressed in the self-portraits done for this introduction, is that the computers are using *them*.

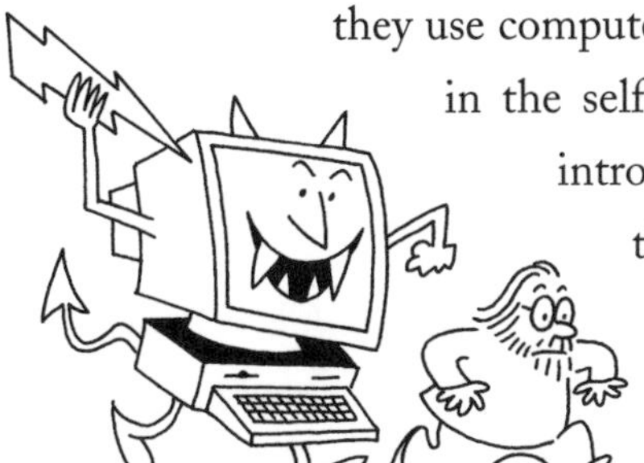

*Charles Barsotti*

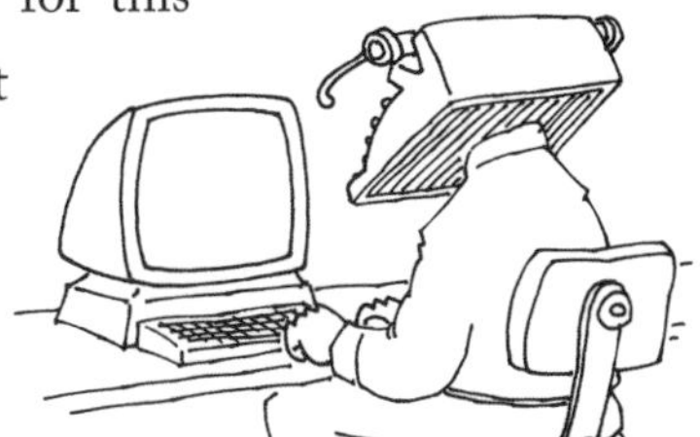

*Jack Ziegler*

But if Ziegler and Barsotti think that a cartoonist needs cutting-edge technology as much as a fish needs a bicycle, Tom (Borg) Cheney clearly envisions a day when a bioengineered flounder wins the Tour de France.

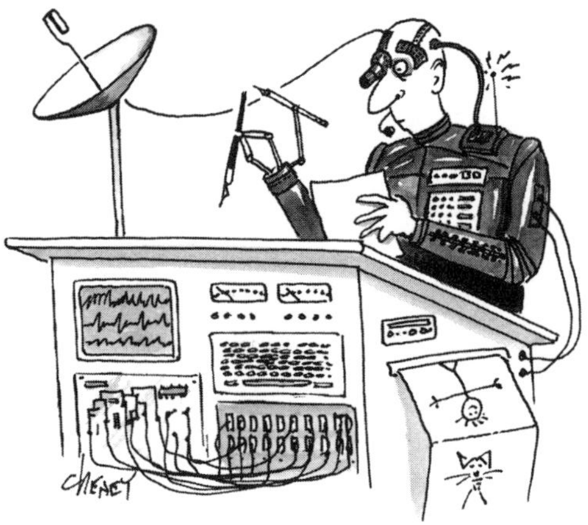

Tom Cheney

Other self-portraits, like those of Mick Stevens and Marisa Acocella, evince a vague sense of foreboding, bringing to mind Yeats's prophetic quote from *The Second Coming,* "Turning and turning in the widening gyre / The falcon cannot hear the falconer; / Nor can he page him." Acocella's drawing further suggests the question "If this is the information age, how come we can't retain any?"

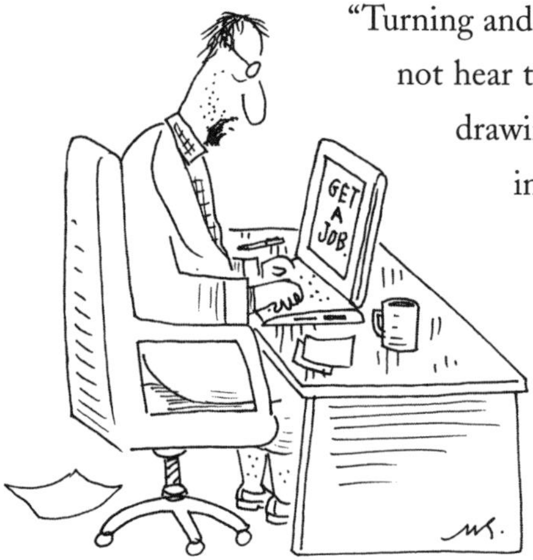
GET A JOB.

*Mick Stevens*

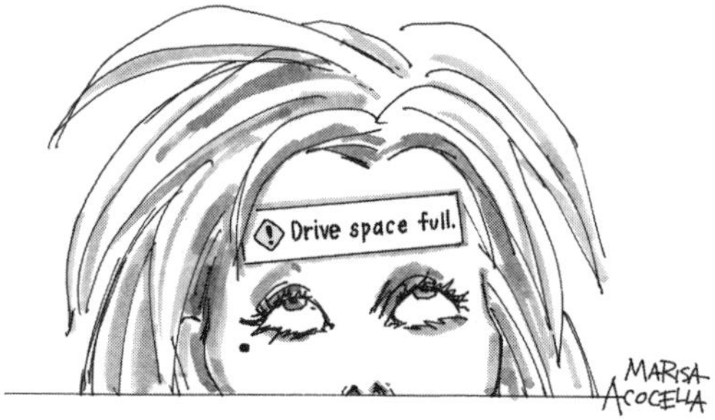
Drive space full.

*Marisa Acocella*

In fact, I happen to know the answer to *that* question. Or at least I know the database the answer is stored in. Now, if only I could remember the password. Clearly, we have become dependent on technology. We can't live without it. How it feels about us, however, is another matter addressed by the one cartoonist I know who actually draws his cartoons on a computer.

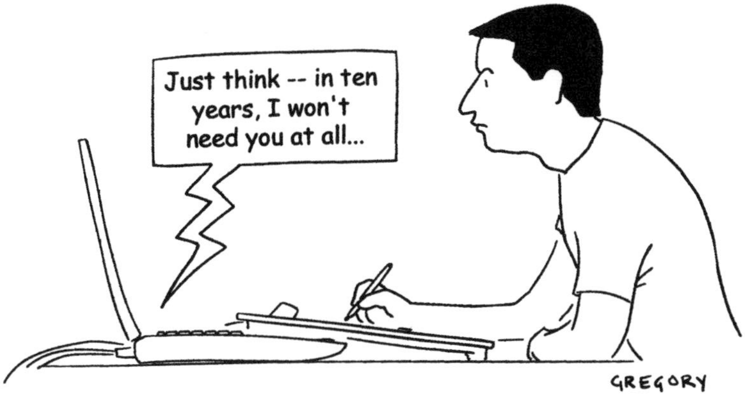
Just think -- in ten years, I won't need you at all...
GREGORY

*Alex Gregory*

Gregory may be right. Time is running out for cartoons done by humans, or even looked at by humans. But don't despair, the carbon-based life-form is still in the driver's seat, even though—as Frank Cotham's portrait shows—it's getting a little crowded up there.

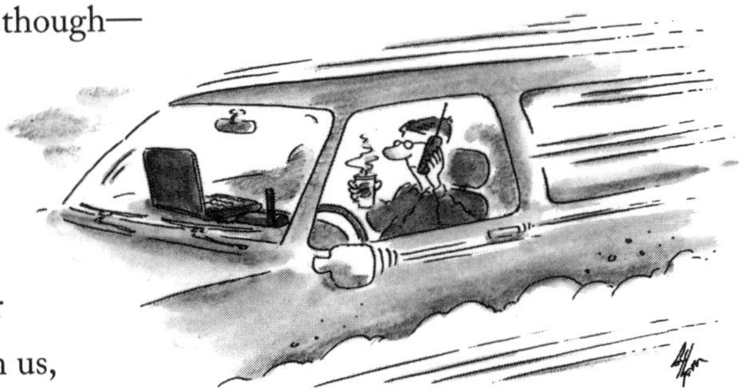

*Frank Cotham*

Meanwhile, my advice is to enjoy the ride, no matter how bumpy. The jokes are on us, about us, and for us, and all you have to do to access 110 of them is to press any key below.

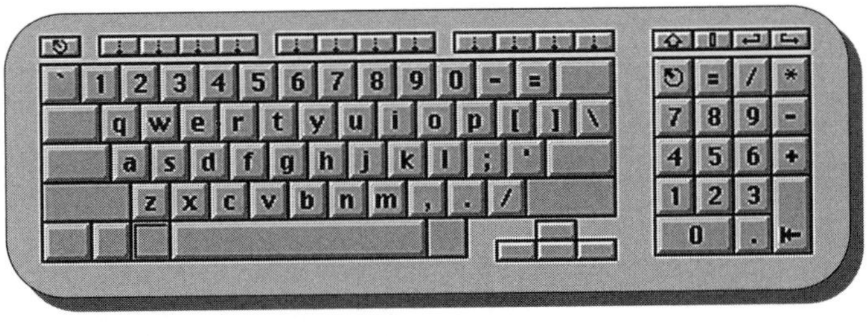

On second thought, just turn the page.

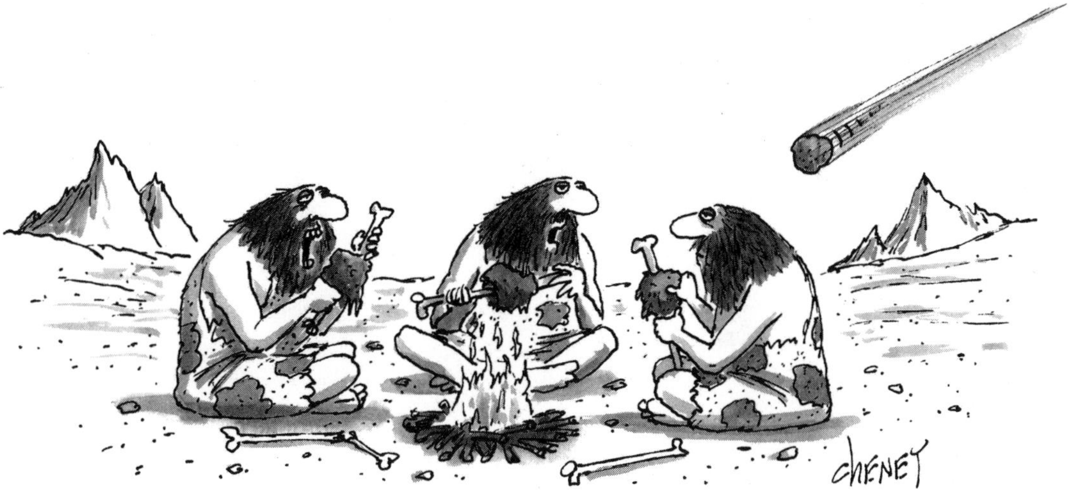
CHENEY

*"You've got mail."*

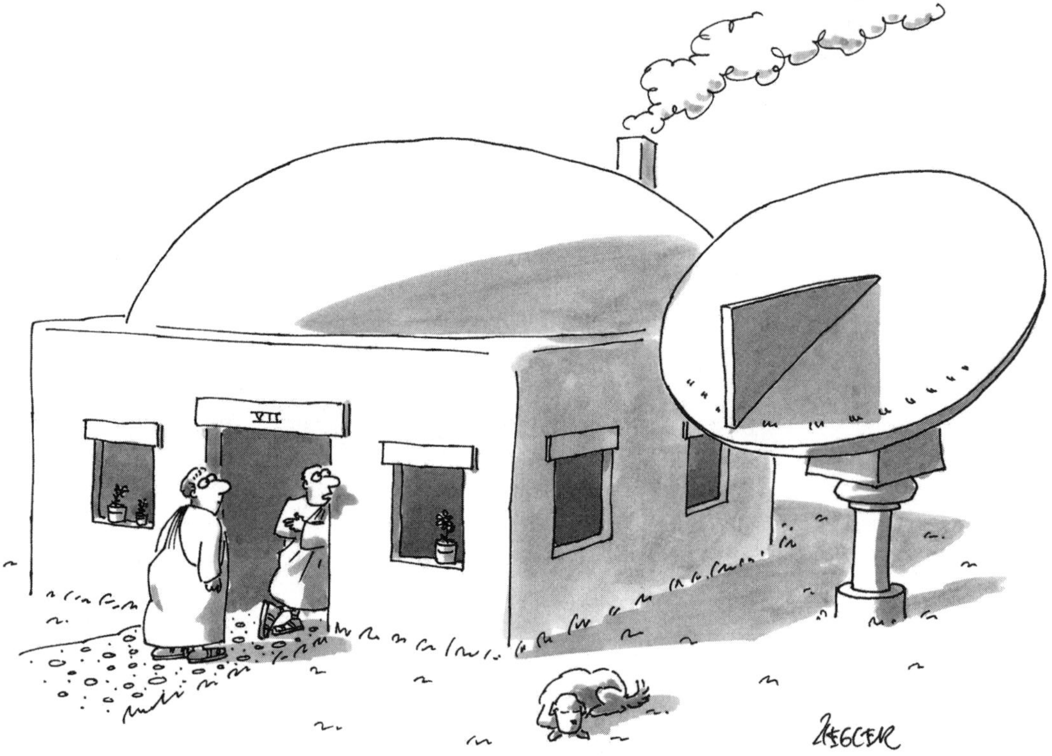
VII

*"Sure, it's an eyesore, but we get better time than anyone else in the neighborhood."*

"First, they do an on-line search."

*"I love the convenience, but the roaming charges are killing me."*

"Oh, like you know something the Internet doesn't know."

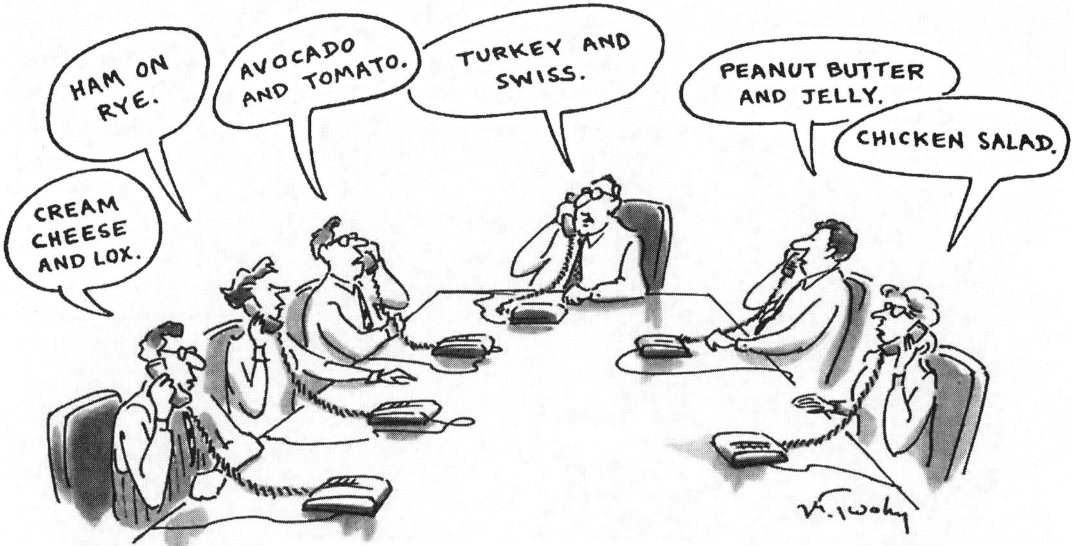
CHICKEN SALAD.
PEANUT BUTTER AND JELLY.
TURKEY AND SWISS.
AVOCADO AND TOMATO.
HAM ON RYE.
CREAM CHEESE AND LOX.

CONFERENCE CALL

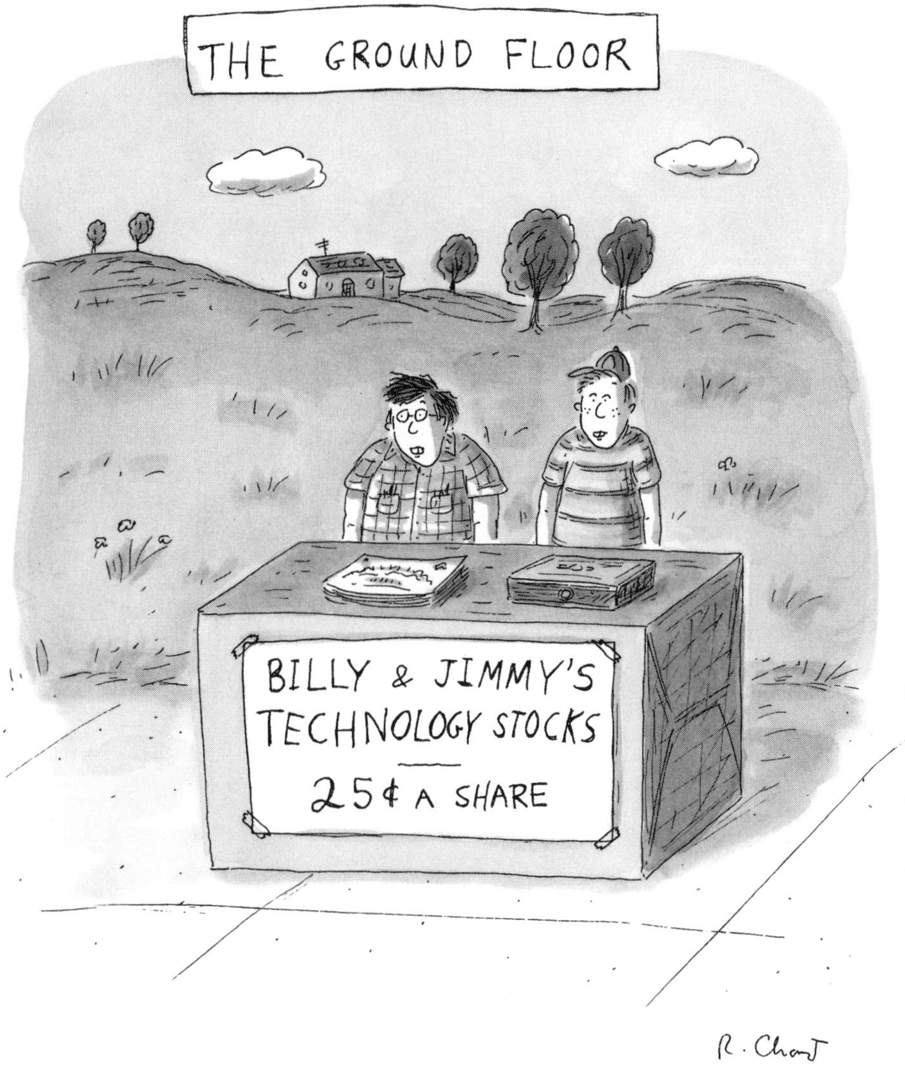
THE GROUND FLOOR
BILLY & JIMMY'S
TECHNOLOGY STOCKS
25¢ A SHARE

*"I'm sorry, Mr. Abbot is away from his desk."*

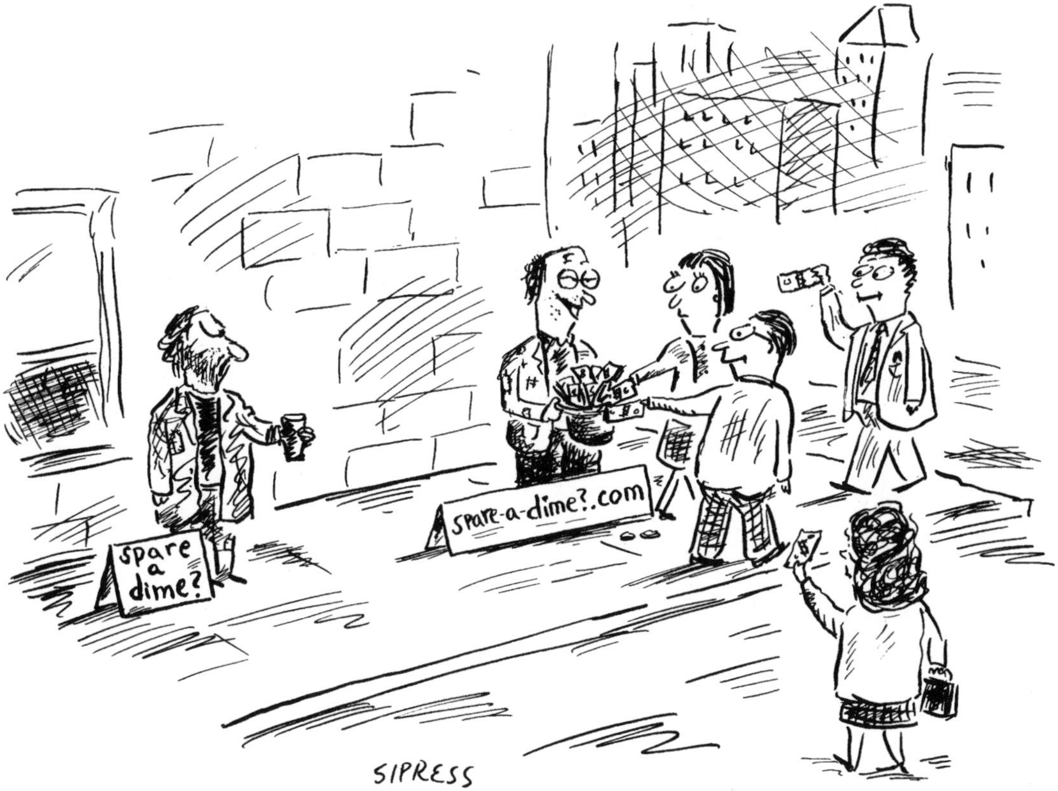
spare
a
dime?
spare-a-dime?.com
SIPRESS

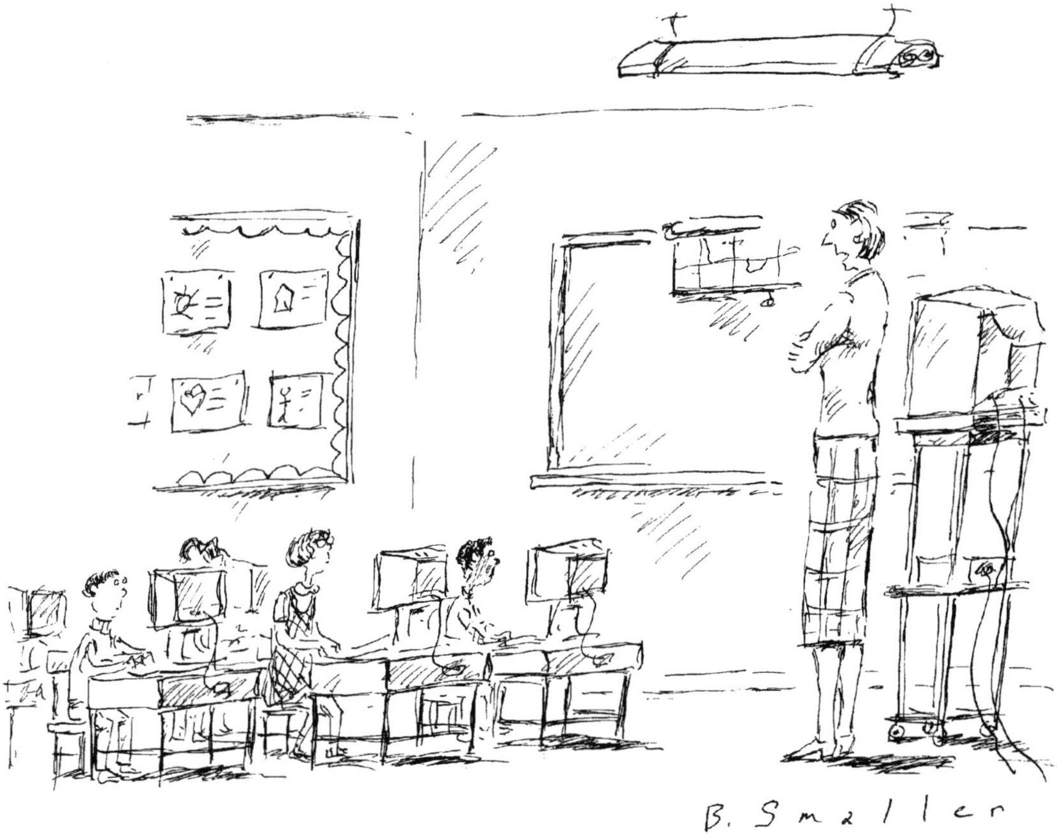
B. Smaller

*"Keep your eyes on your own screen."*

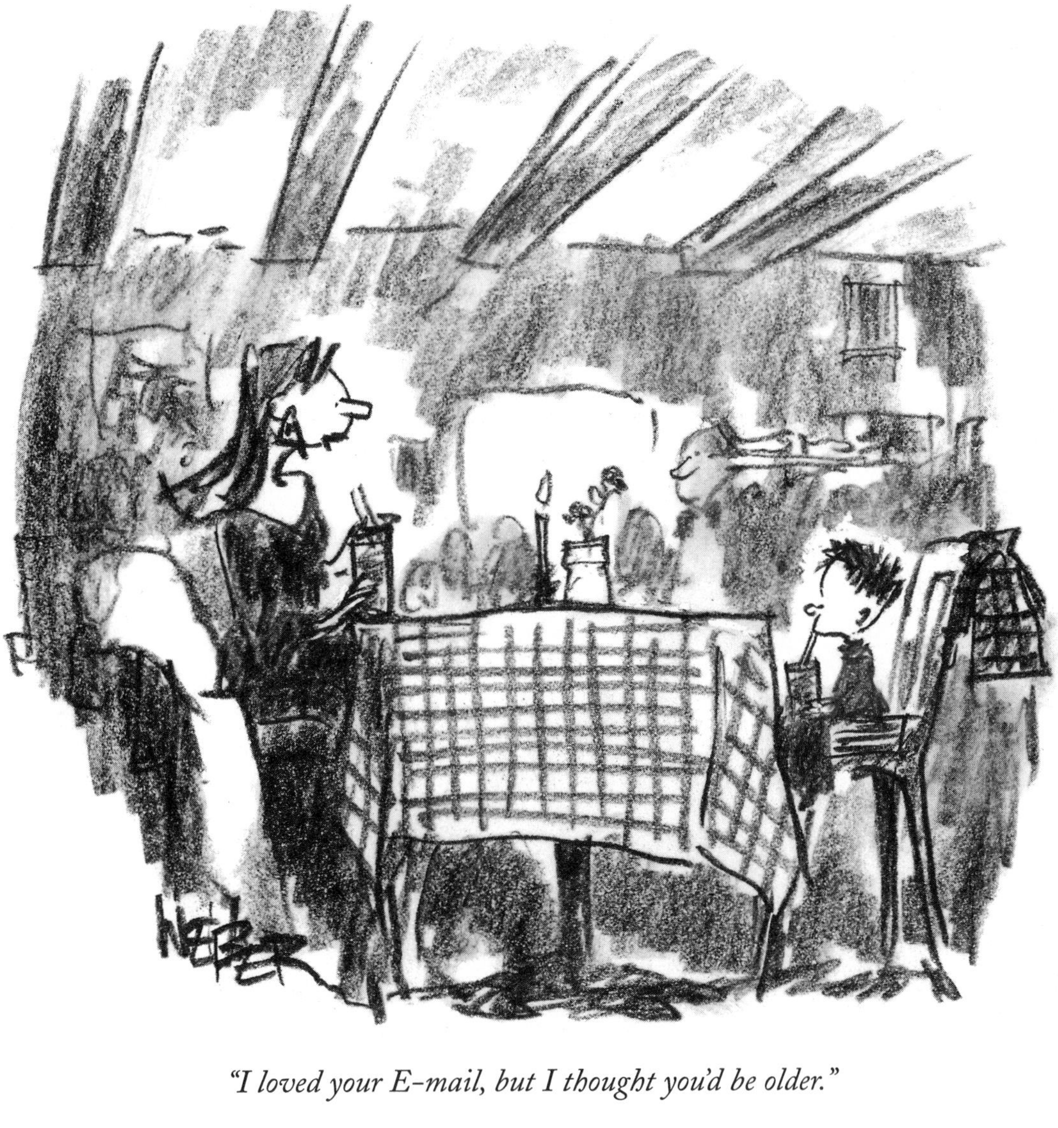
WEBER

*"I loved your E-mail, but I thought you'd be older."*

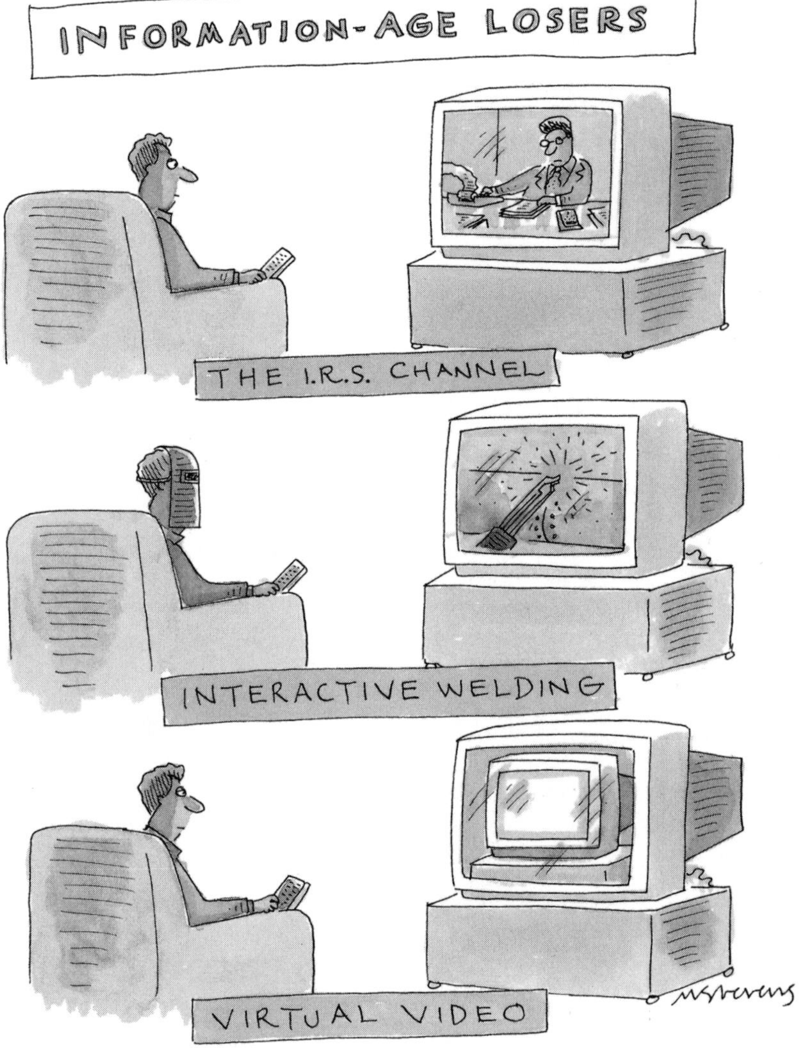
INFORMATION-AGE LOSERS
THE I.R.S. CHANNEL
INTERACTIVE WELDING
VIRTUAL VIDEO
MStevens

*"All I'm saying is <u>now</u> is the time to develop the technology to deflect an asteroid."*

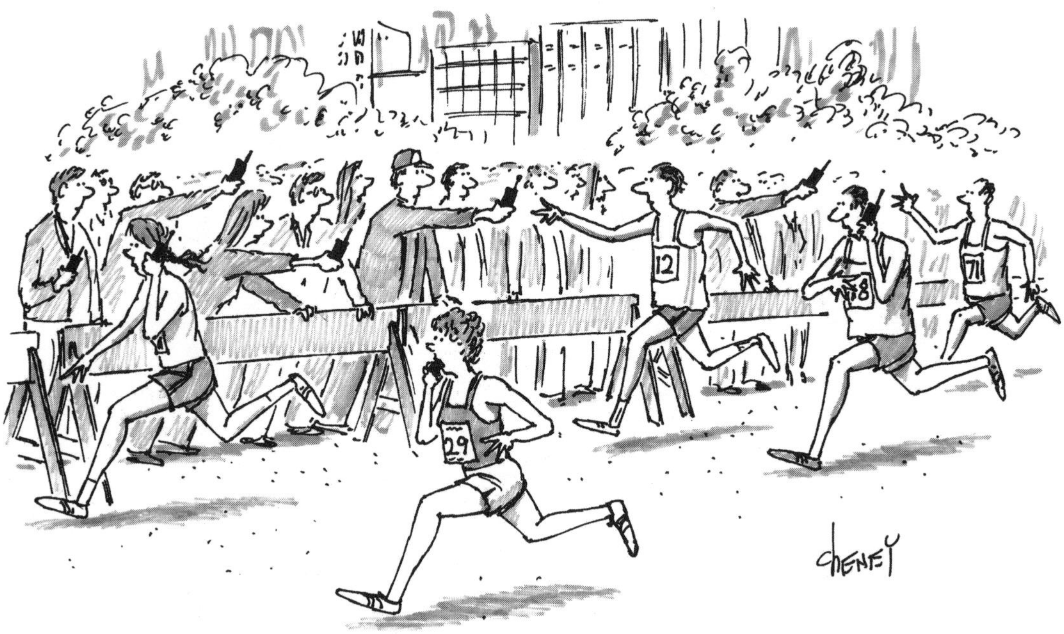
12
29
8
71
CHENEY

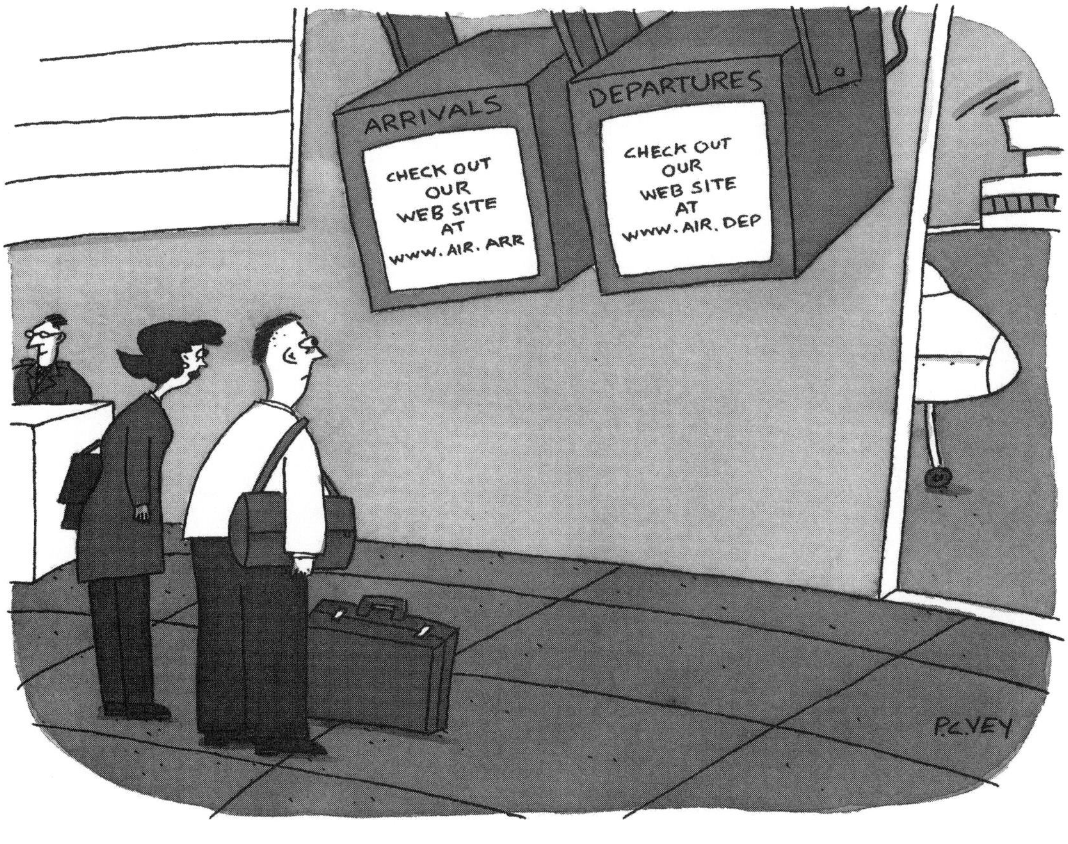
ARRIVALS
CHECK OUT OUR WEB SITE AT WWW.AIR.ARR
DEPARTURES
CHECK OUT OUR WEB SITE AT WWW.AIR.DEP
P.C.VEY

"You see that dark, spooky image on the screen? That's your credit history coming back to haunt you."

"You can access me by saying simply 'Agnes.' It is not necessary to add 'dot com.'"

"Hello. I'm a first-time caller."

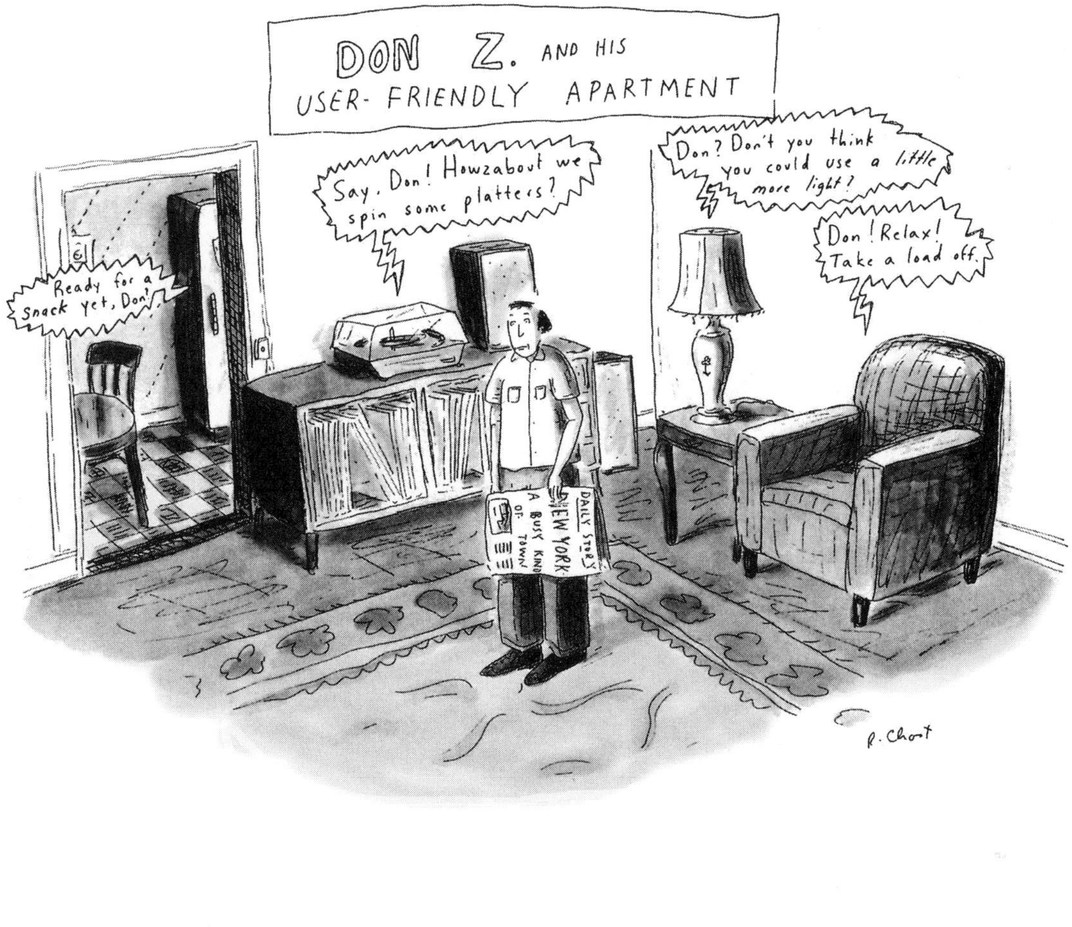
DON Z. AND HIS USER-FRIENDLY APARTMENT
Ready for a snack yet, Don?
Say, Don! Howzabout we spin some platters?
Don? Don't you think you could use a little more light?
Don! Relax! Take a load off.
DAILY STORY
NEW YORK: A BUSY KIND OF TOWN!
R. Chast

*"We are all fed up with you
doing these damn power breakfasts at home."*

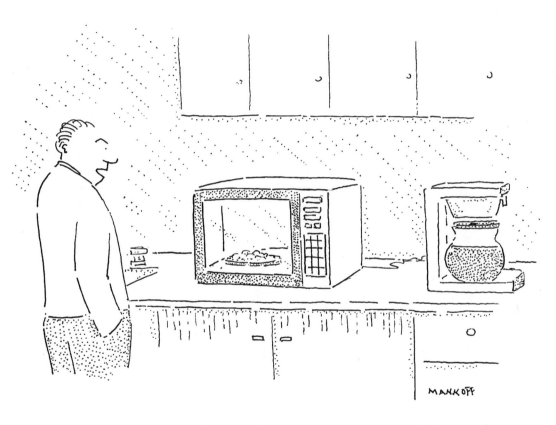

"No, I don't want to play chess. I just want you to reheat the lasagna."

"And then I met some computer people who could make it look as if I were talking."

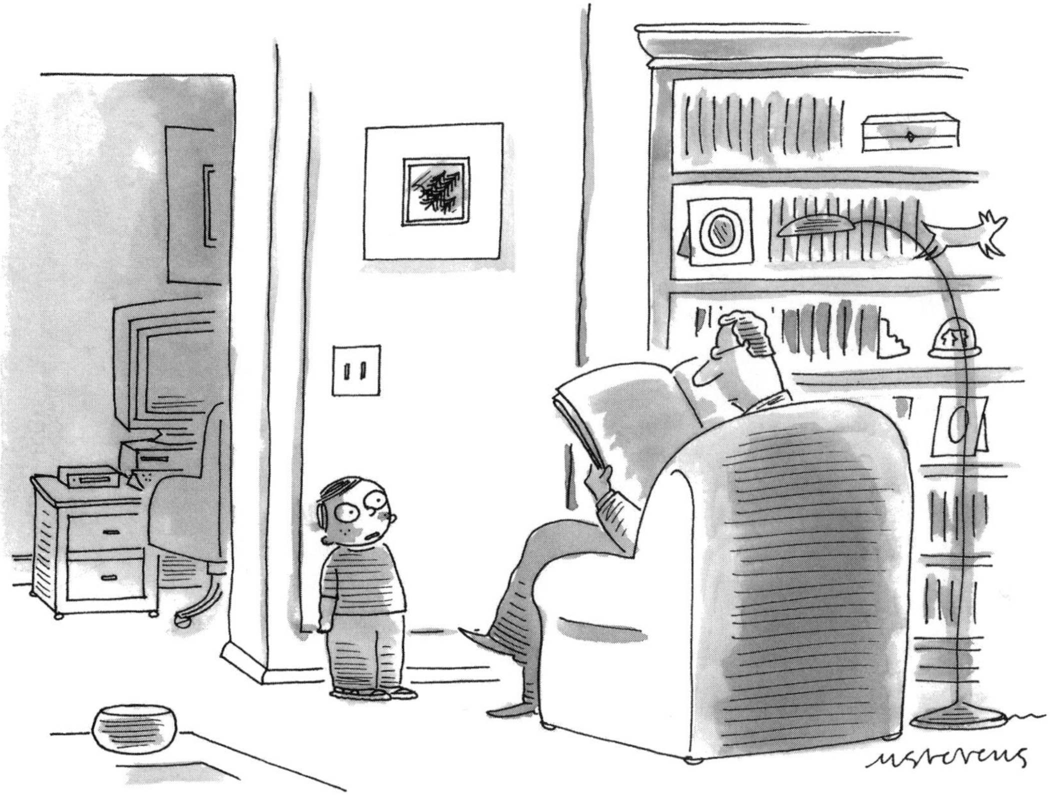

MStevens


*"Dad, can I borrow your password tonight?"*

"It must be his beeper."

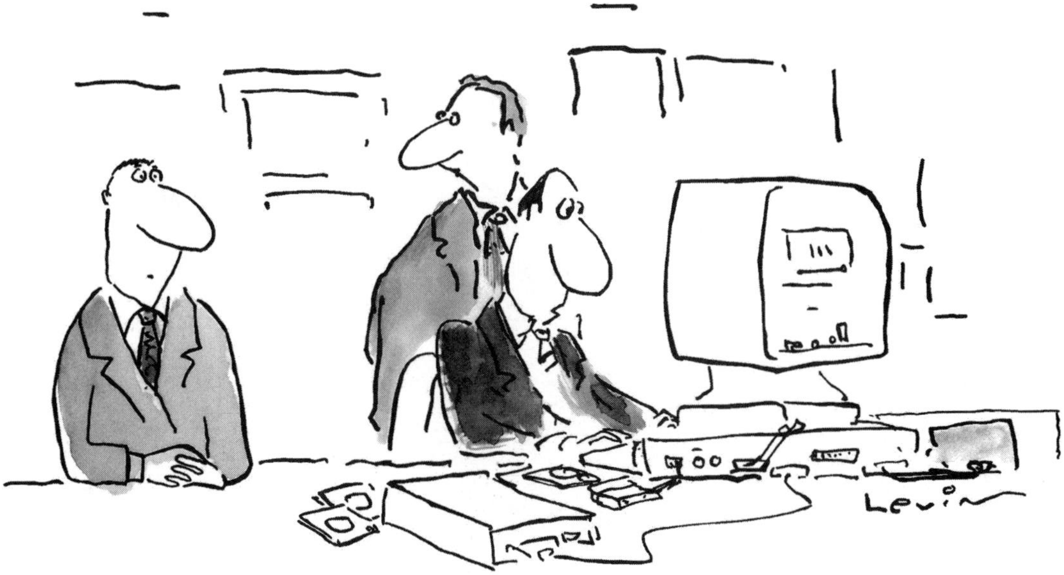
Levin

*"I haven't the slightest idea who he is. He came bundled with the software."*

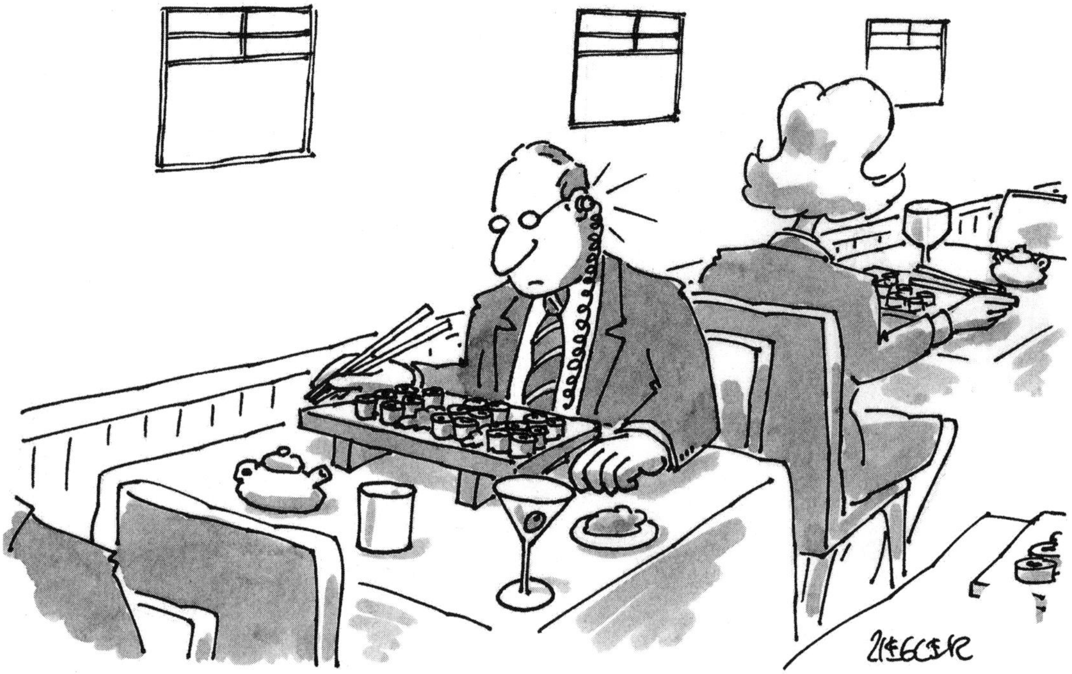
ZIEGLER

*"From right to left, you have your tekkamaki, your futomaki, and then your yamaimo roll. The little pile of pink stuff is ginger, the green one's wasabi. And, of course, you already recognize your vodka martini."*

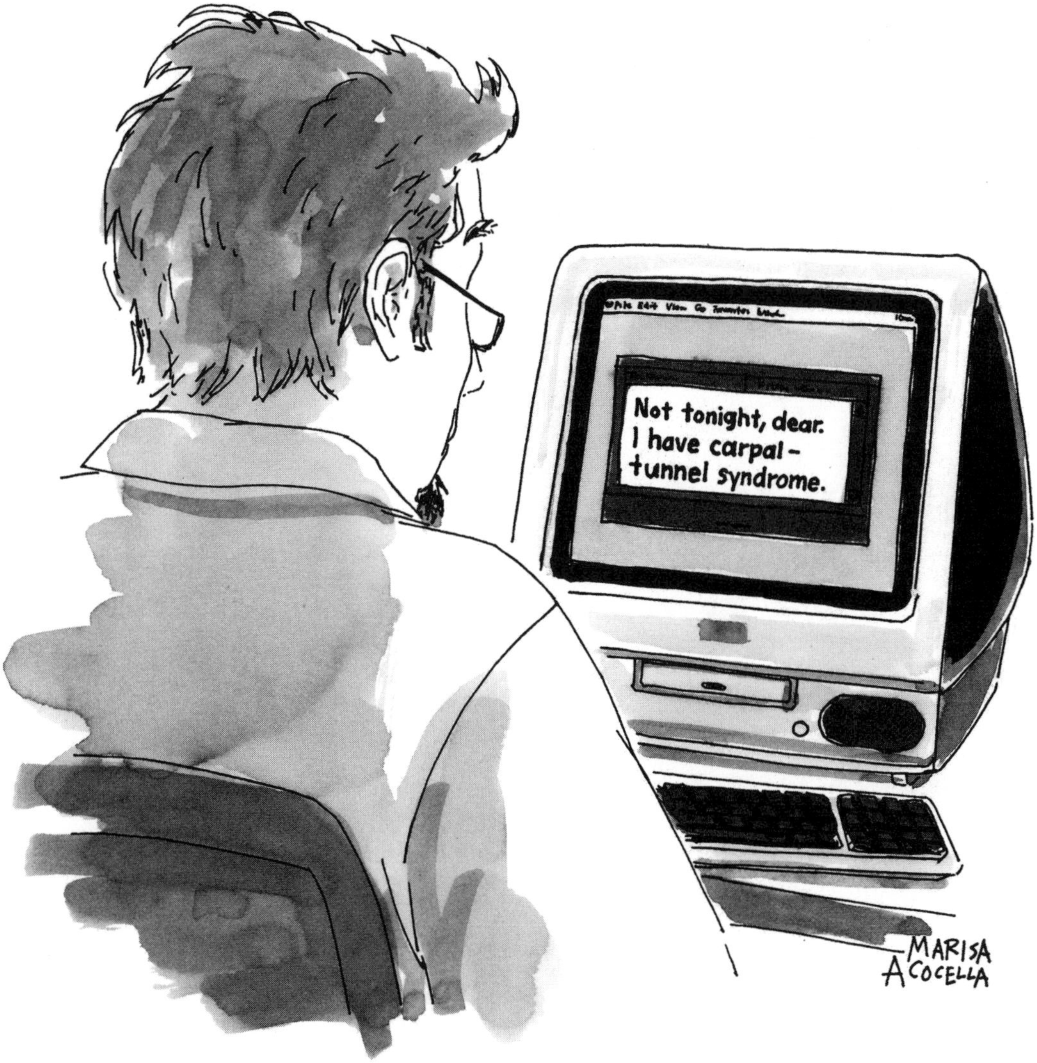
Not tonight, dear.
I have carpal-
tunnel syndrome.
MARISA
ACOCELLA

*"Alright, Ms. Ramsey, send in the clones."*

"The gods must be on-line tonight."

"Nothing important—nothing on fax, nothing on voice mail, nothing on the Internet. Just, you know, handwritten stuff."

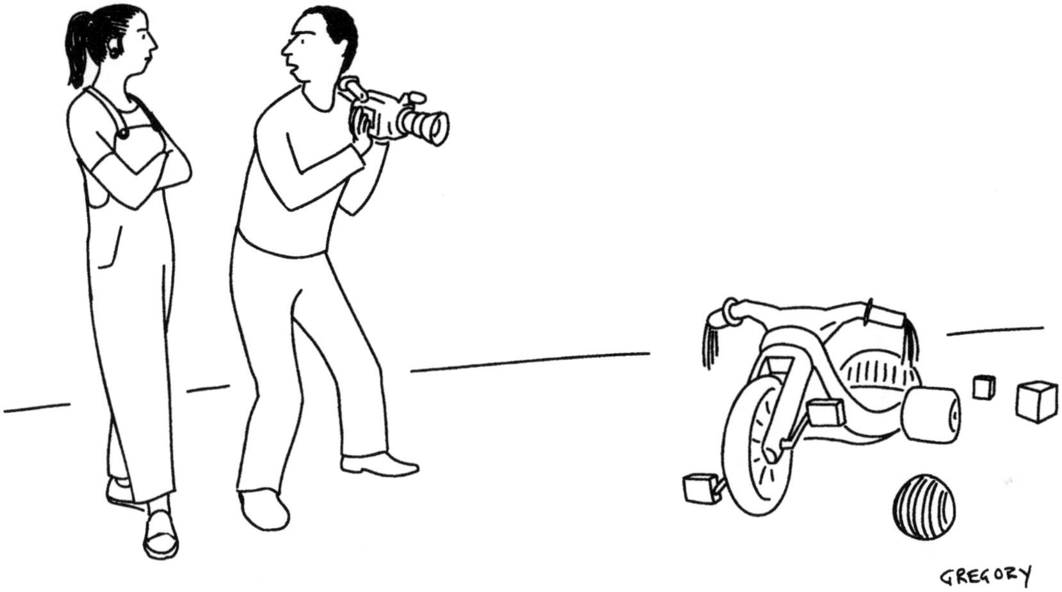
GREGORY

*"I figure we can blue-screen the kids in later."*

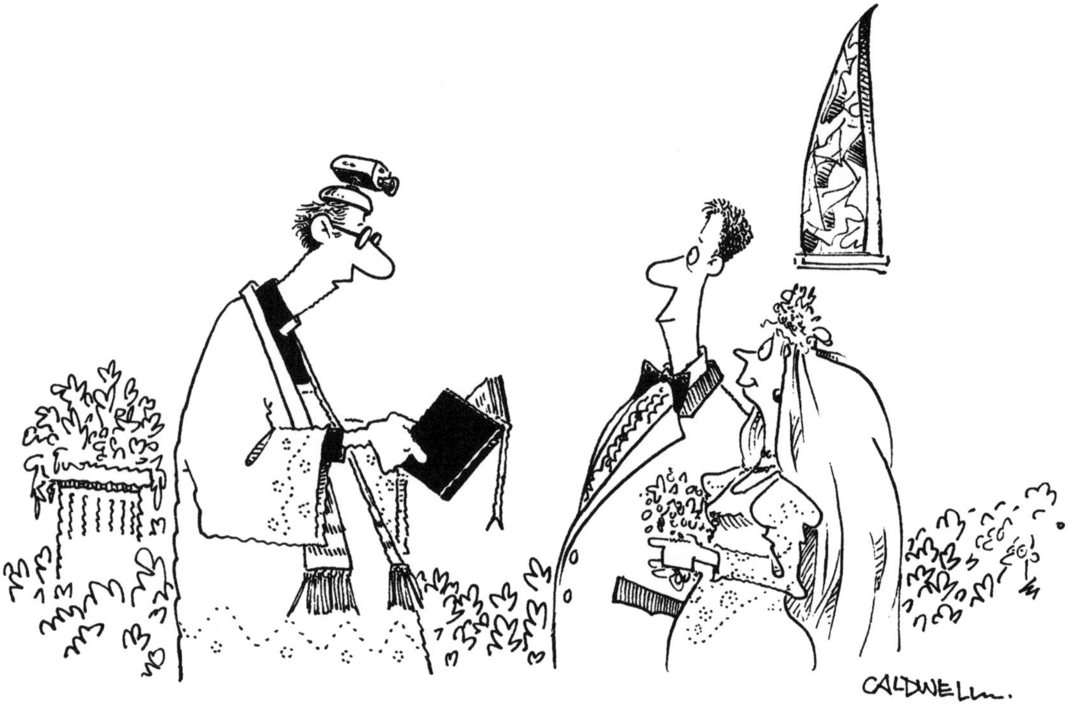
CALDWELL

*"If there is anyone who objects to this union, either here or on the Internet, speak now or forever hold your peace."*

*"Well, being single and a robot, I'm able to put in a lot of overtime."*

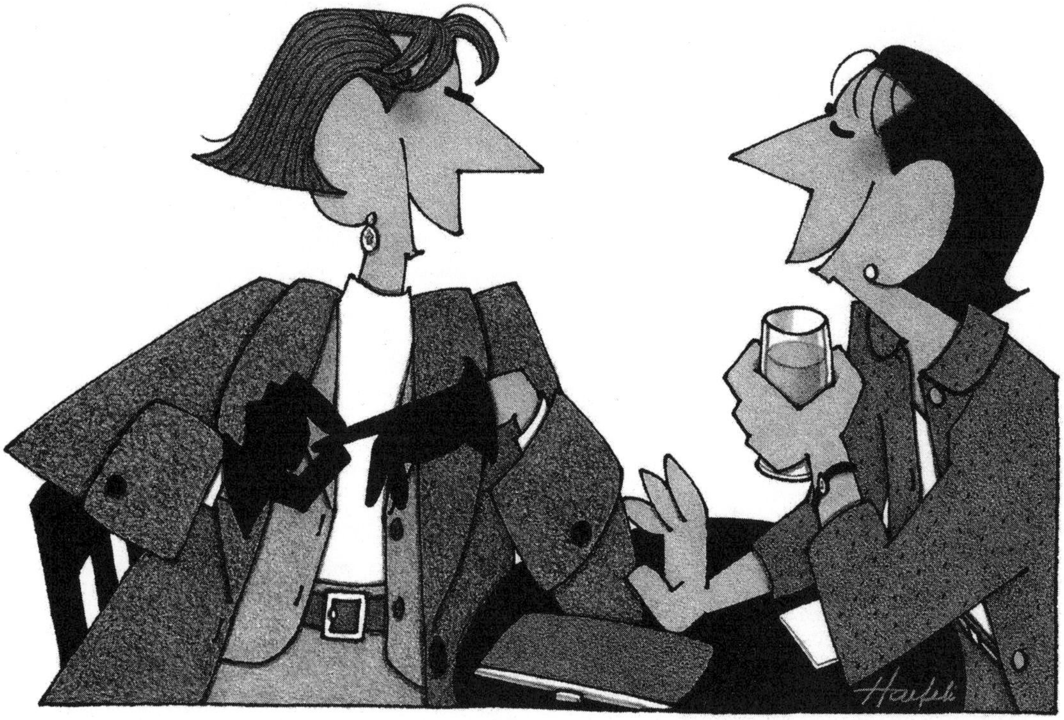
Haefeli

*"I sold his unlisted phone number to telemarketers."*

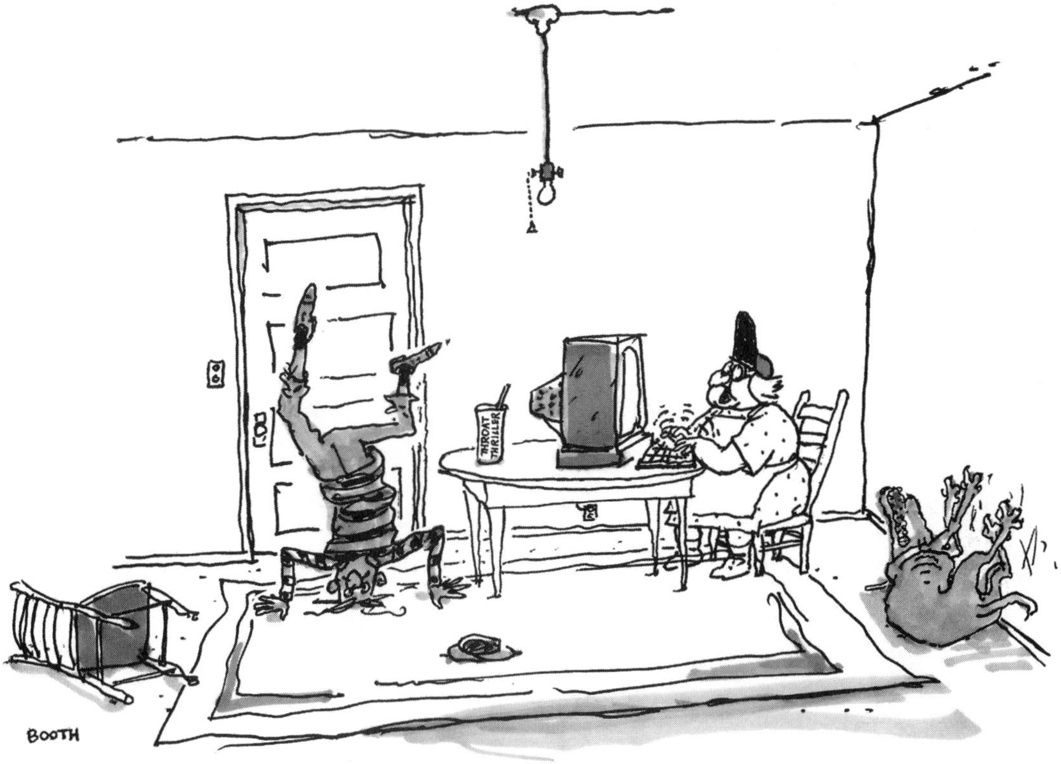
THROAT THRILLER
BOOTH

*"Just for kicks, Leon, let's shut down the F.B.I. again."*

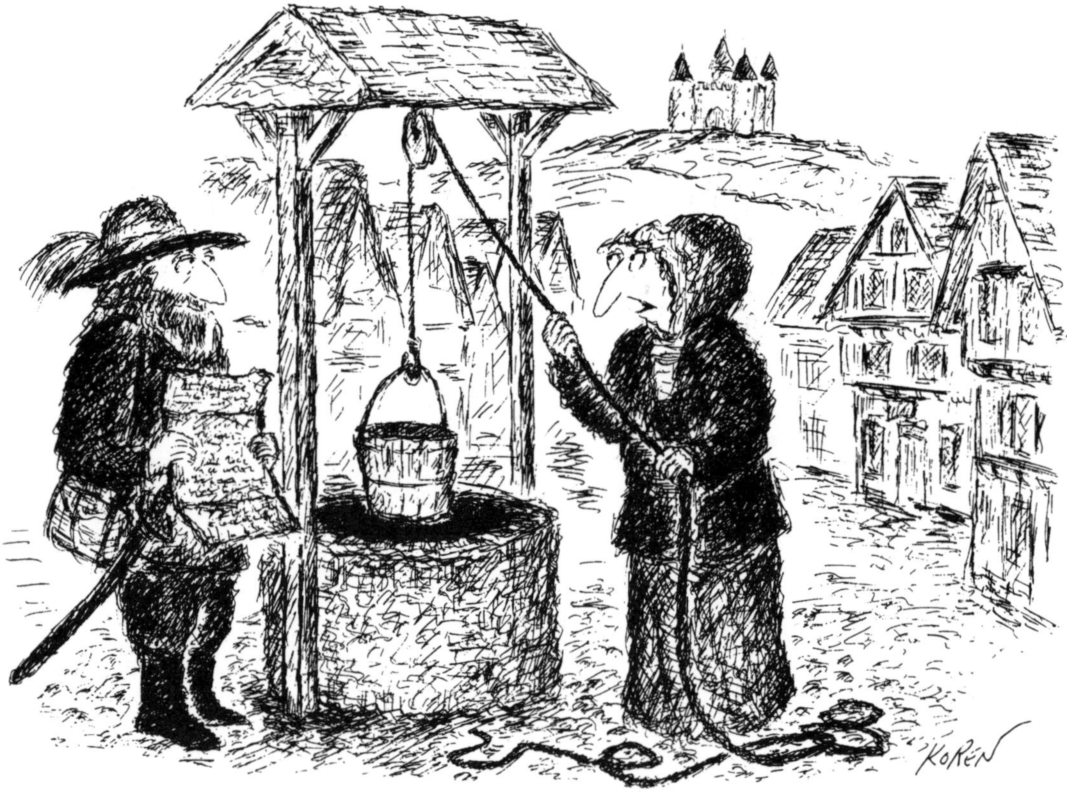
KOREN

*"First, let me pull up your file."*

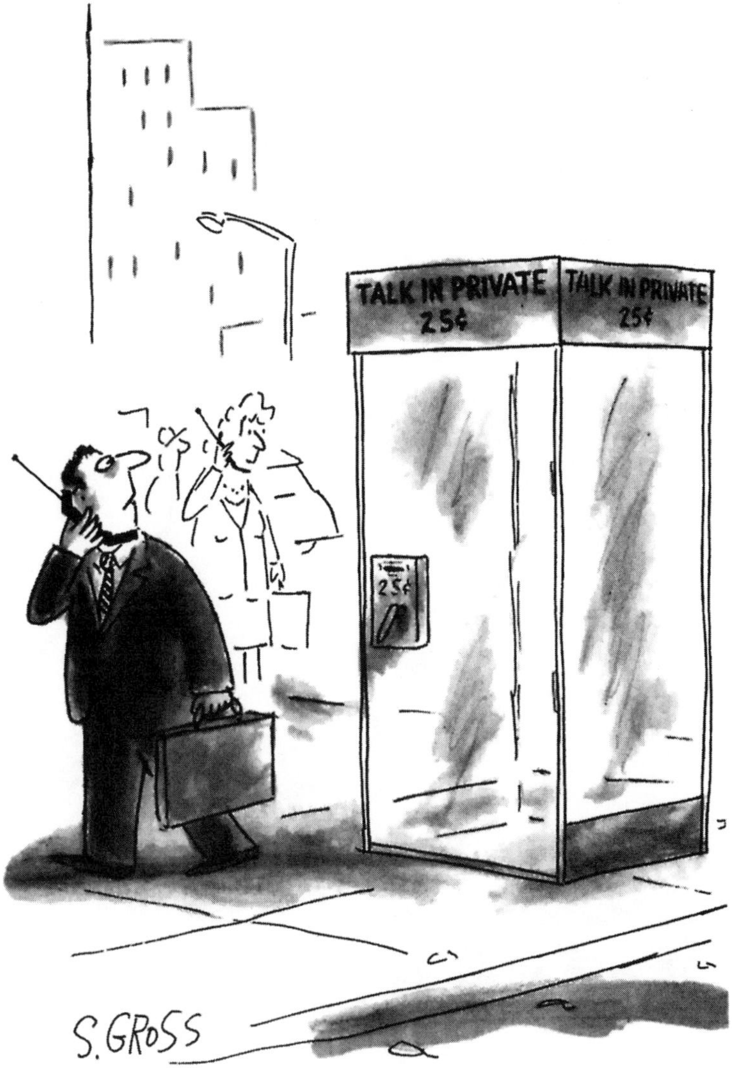
TALK IN PRIVATE
25¢
TALK IN PRIVATE
25¢
25¢
S. GROSS

"*Very nice résumé. Leave a sample of your DNA with my secretary.*"

"*This is so cool! I'm flying this thing completely on my Palm pilot!*"

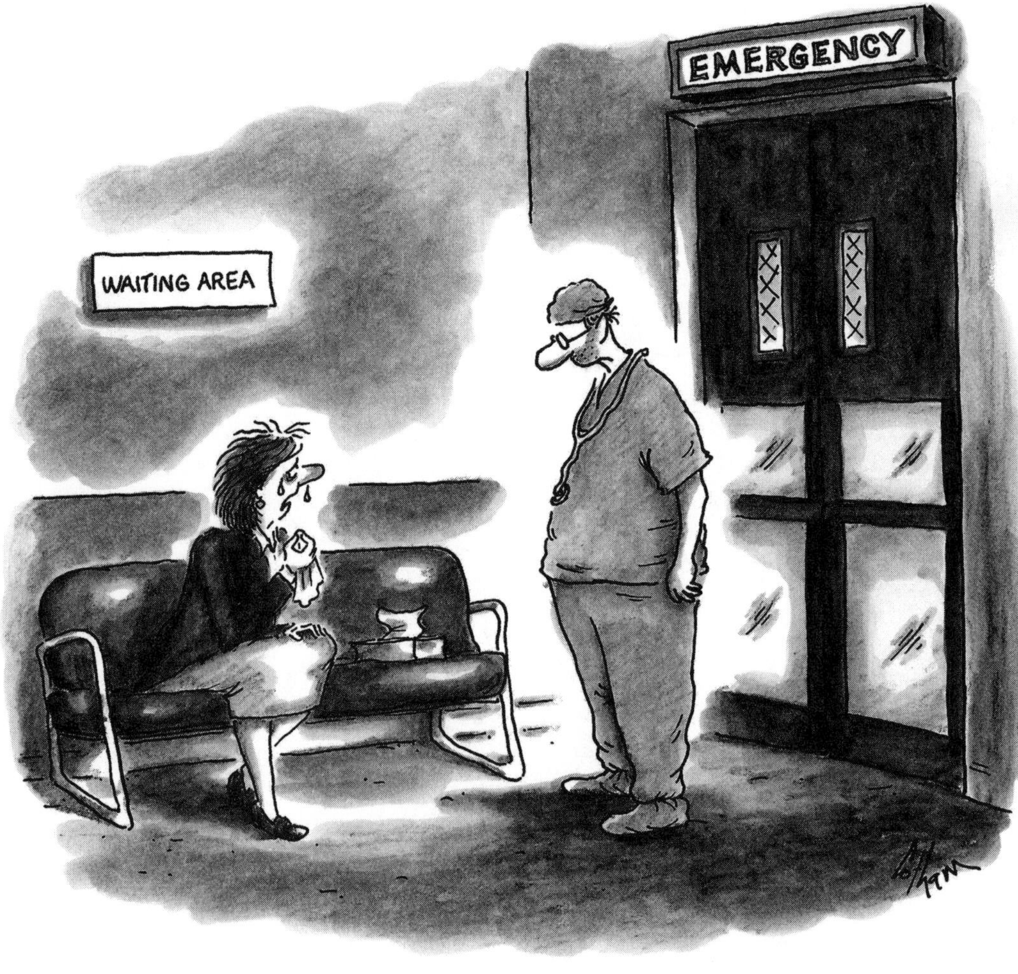
EMERGENCY
WAITING AREA

*"I already know he's gone—it's been on the Internet."*

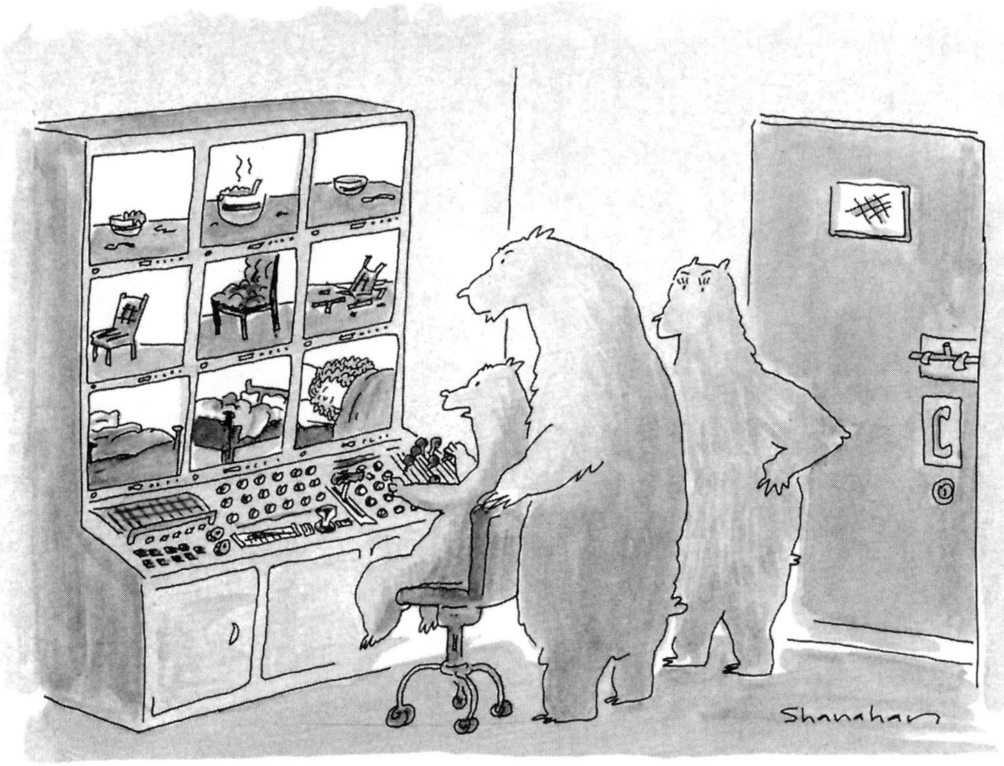
Shanahan

*"Someone's been sleeping in my bed, too, and there she is on Screen Nine!"*

"You are entitled to one call, one fax, or one e-mail."

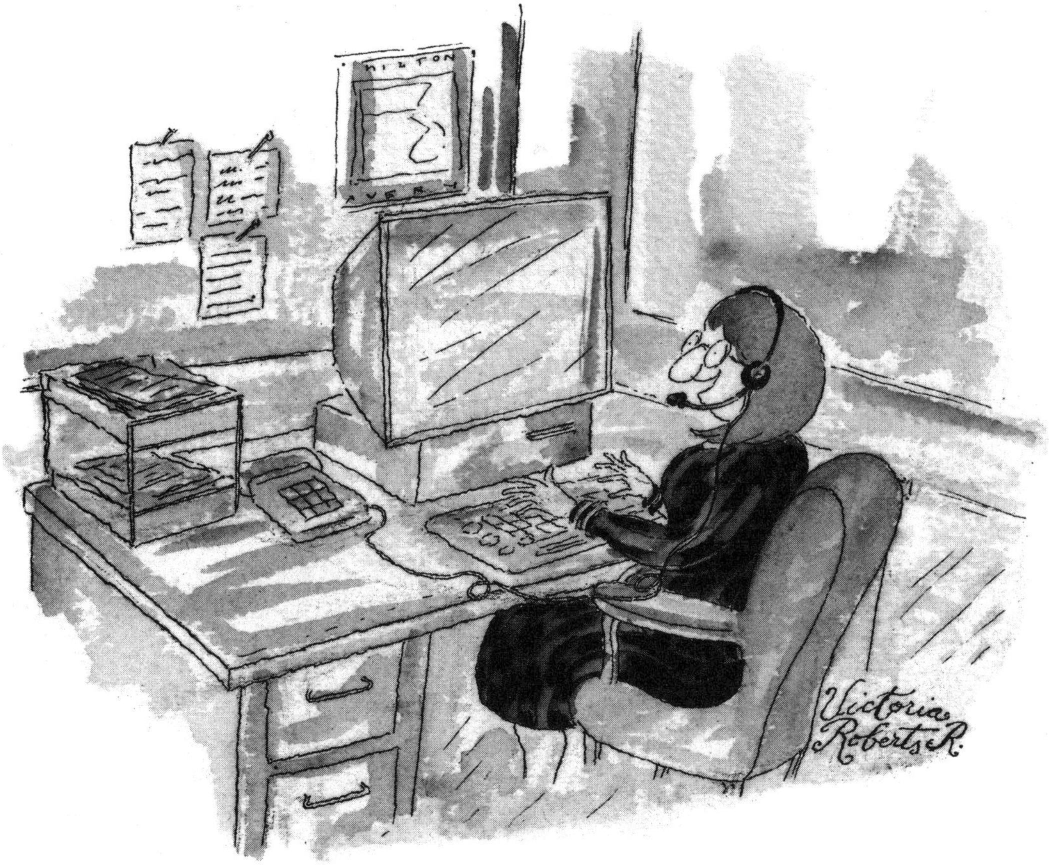
AVERY
Victoria Roberts R.

*"Can I call you back? I'm shopping."*

*"Are we thinking here, or is this just so much pointing and clicking?"*

*Please listen carefully, as my menu options have changed.*"

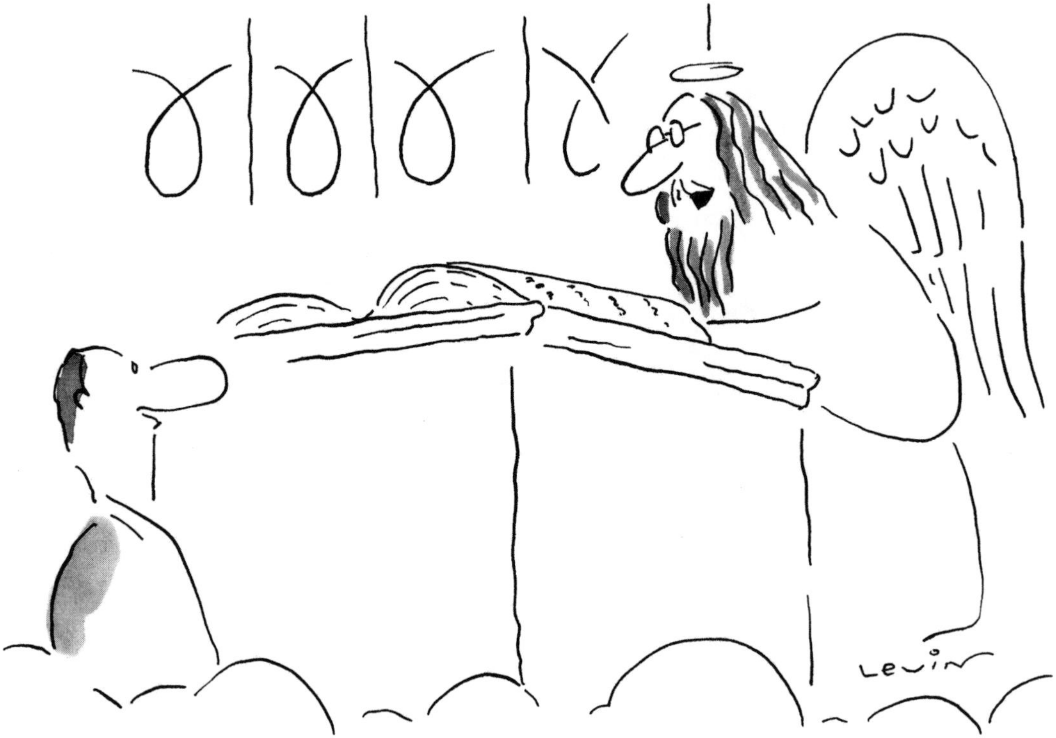
LEVIN

*"User name and password?"*

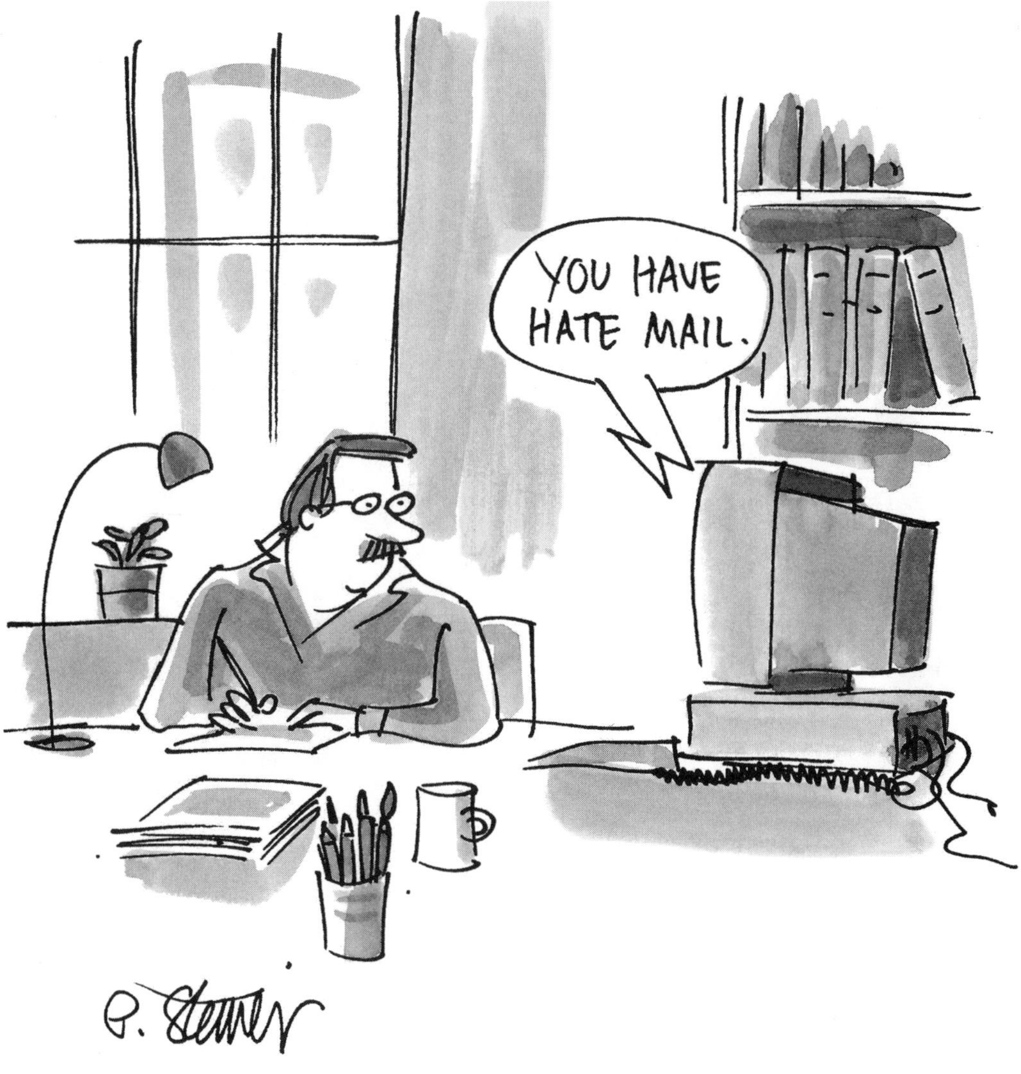
YOU HAVE HATE MAIL.

*"Oh, Lord! We forgot to invite any content providers."*

"Marry me, Virginia. My genes are excellent and, as yet, unpatented."

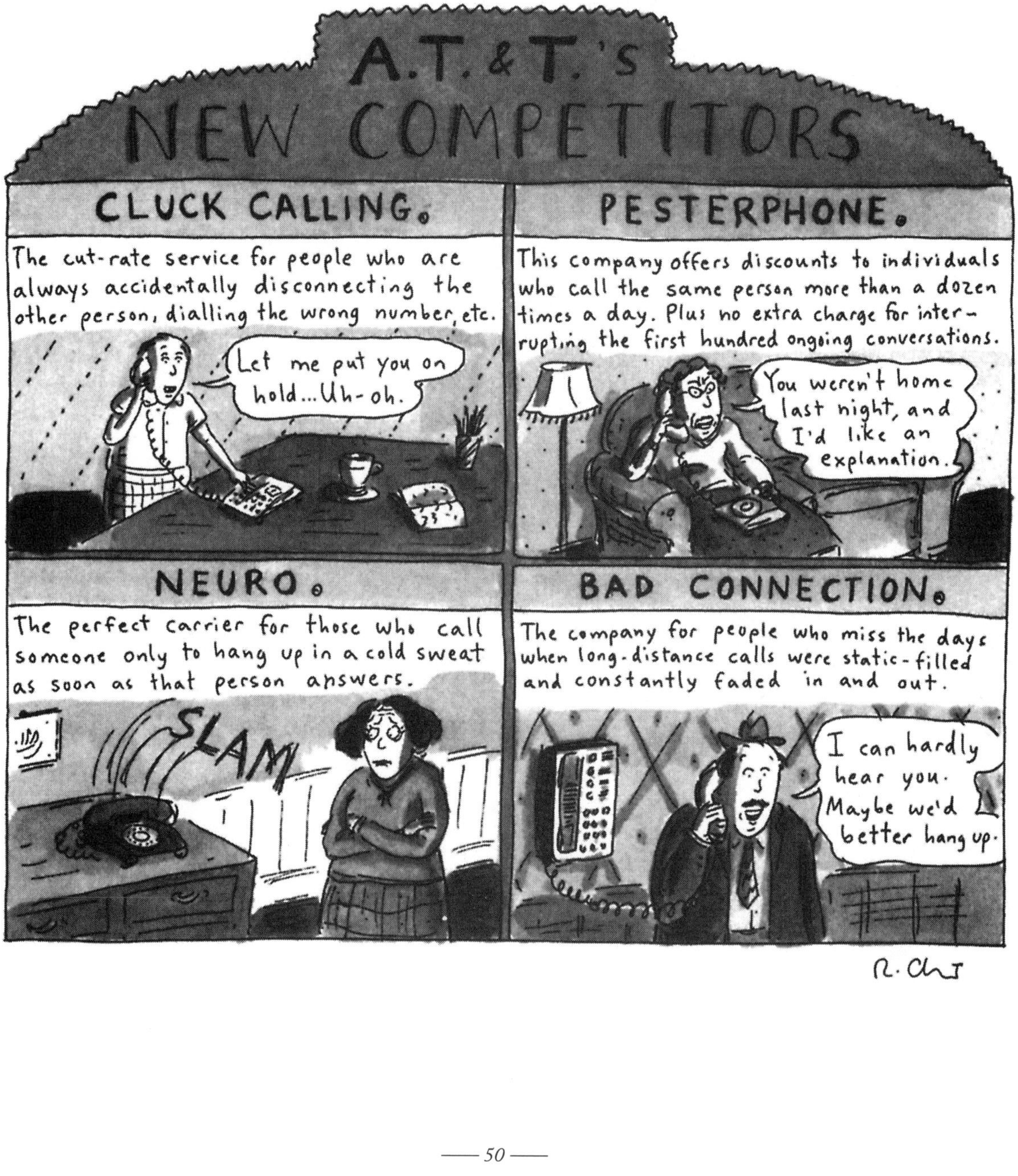
A.T.&T.'s
NEW COMPETITORS
CLUCK CALLING.
The cut-rate service for people who are always accidentally disconnecting the other person, dialling the wrong number, etc.
Let me put you on hold... Uh-oh.
PESTERPHONE.
This company offers discounts to individuals who call the same person more than a dozen times a day. Plus no extra charge for interrupting the first hundred ongoing conversations.
You weren't home last night, and I'd like an explanation.
NEURO.
The perfect carrier for those who call someone only to hang up in a cold sweat as soon as that person answers.
SLAM
BAD CONNECTION.
The company for people who miss the days when long-distance calls were static-filled and constantly faded in and out.
I can hardly hear you. Maybe we'd better hang up.

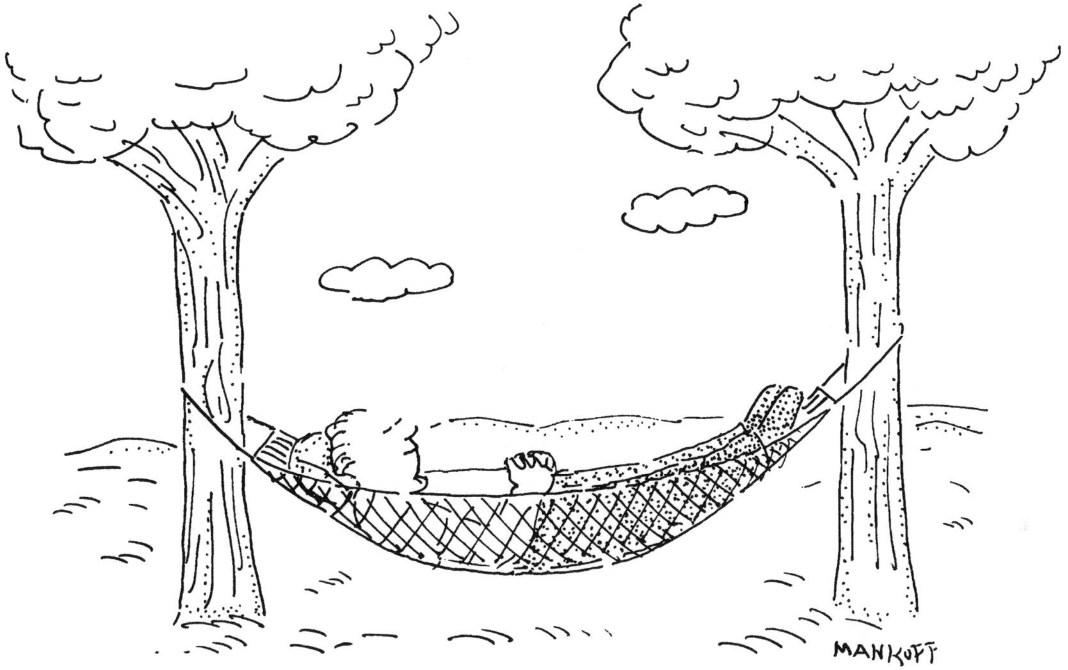
MANKOFF

AMERICA OFF-LINE

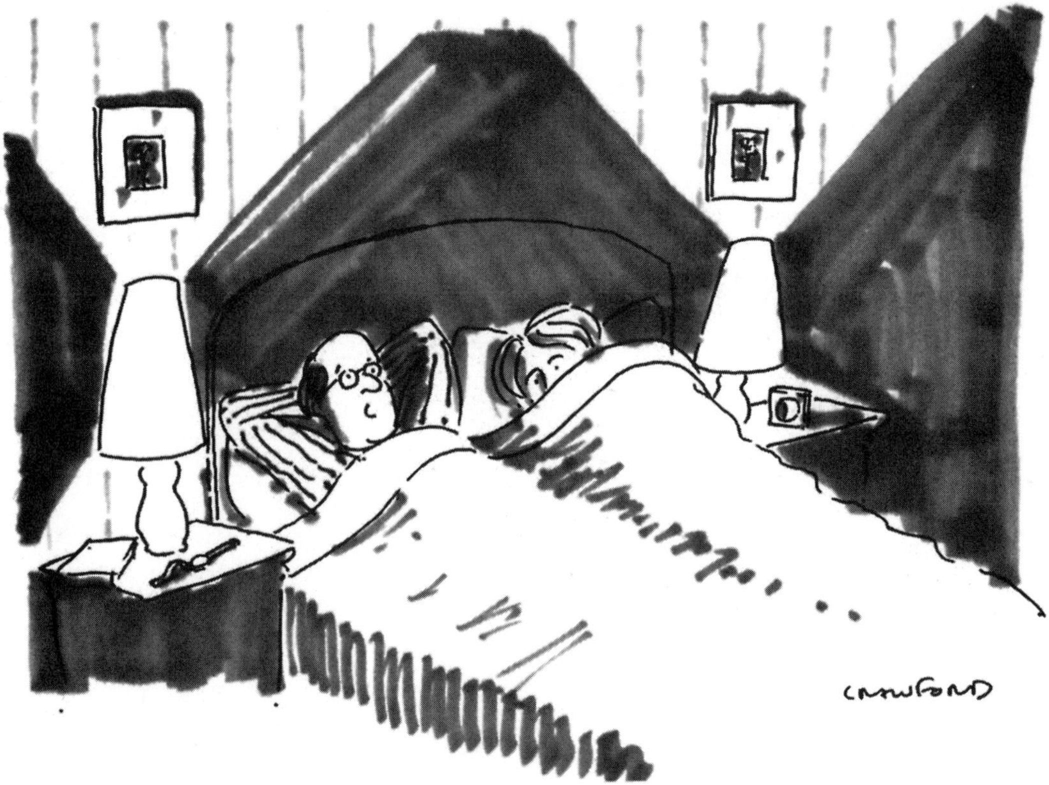
CRAWFORD

*"Not tonight, hon. It'll just wreak havoc with the motion sensors again."*

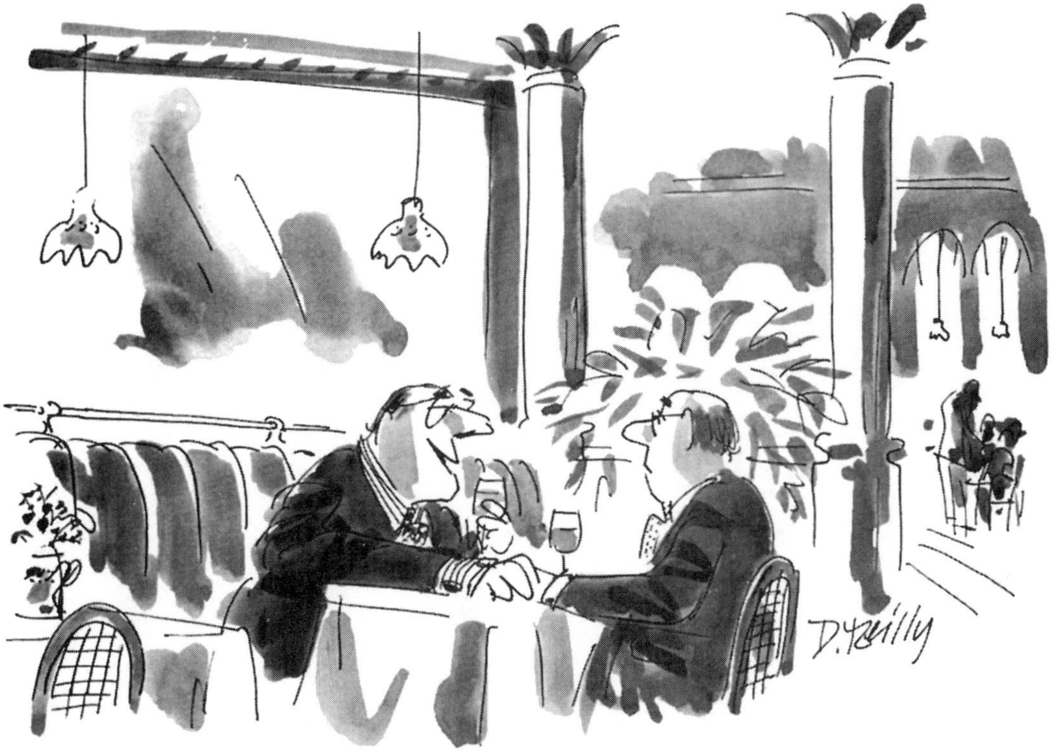
D.Reilly

*"Trust me Mort—no electronic-communications superhighway, no matter how vast and sophisticated, will ever replace the art of the schmooze."*

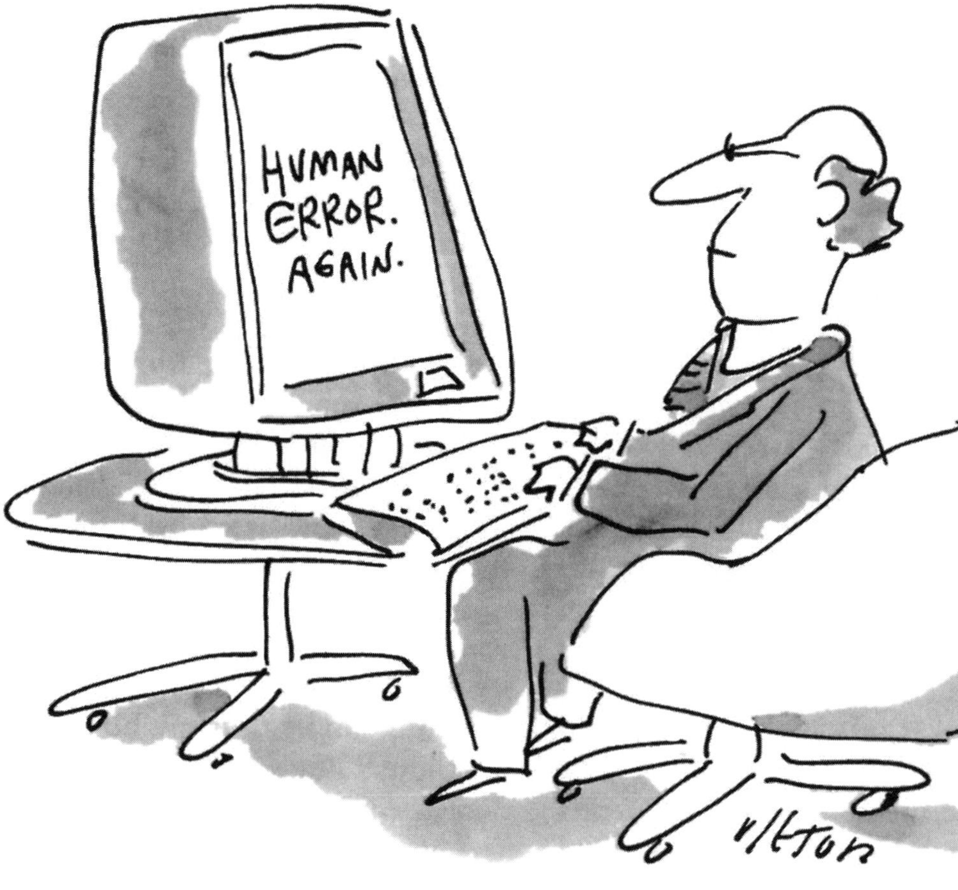
HUMAN
ERROR.
AGAIN.

*"I'd like to say 'Hi' to my granddaddy in Roswell, New Mexico."*

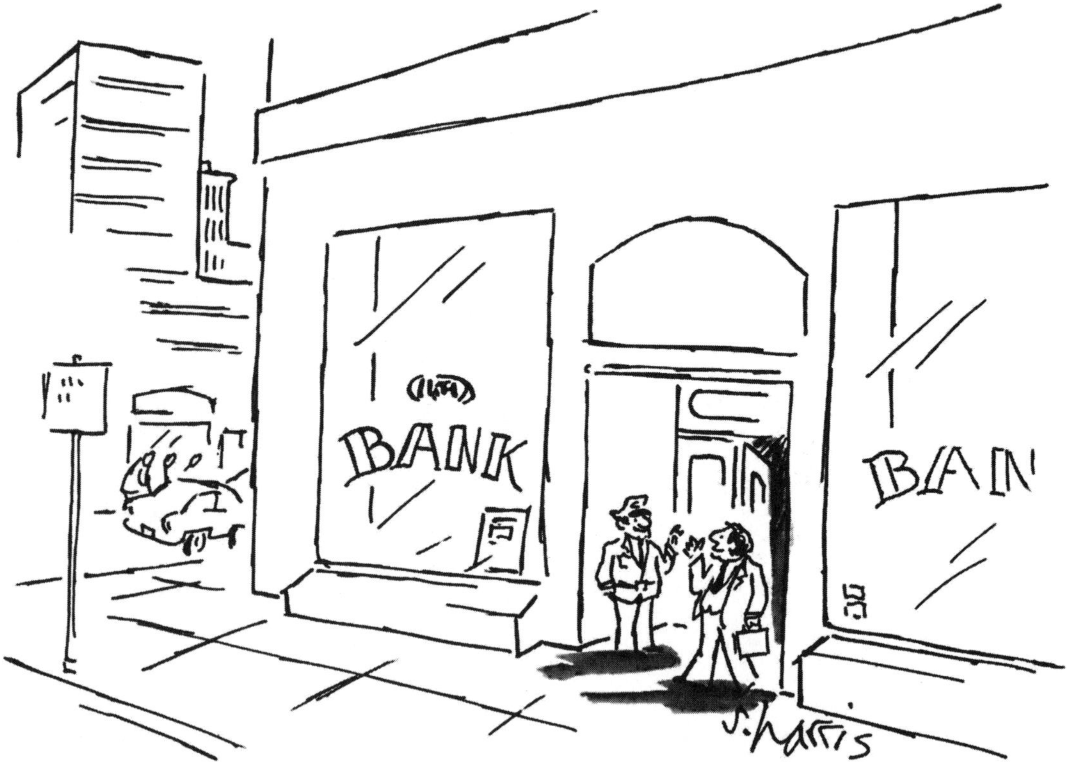
BANK
BAN
S. Harris

PERPETRATOR OF A DARING DAYLIGHT ILLEGAL ELECTRONIC TRANSFER OF FUNDS FLEEING THE SCENE OF THE CRIME

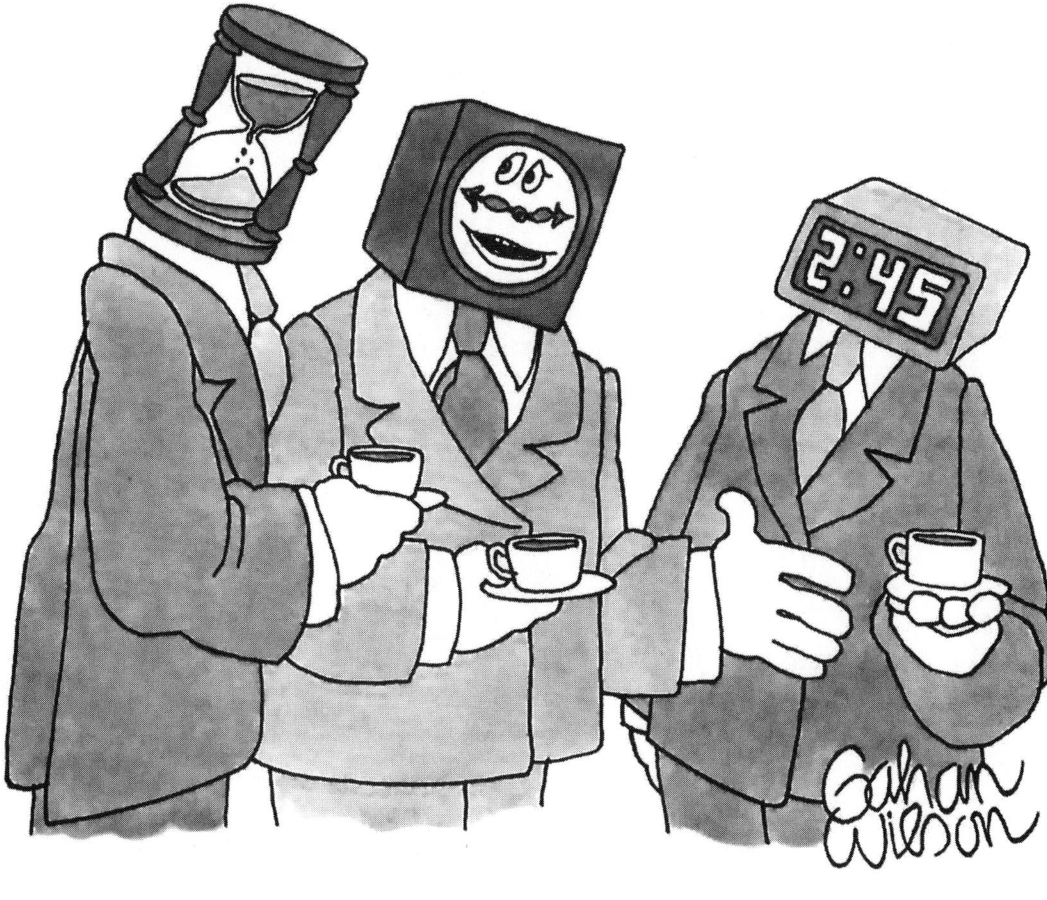
2:45
Gahan Wilson

*"Basically, we're all trying to say the same thing."*

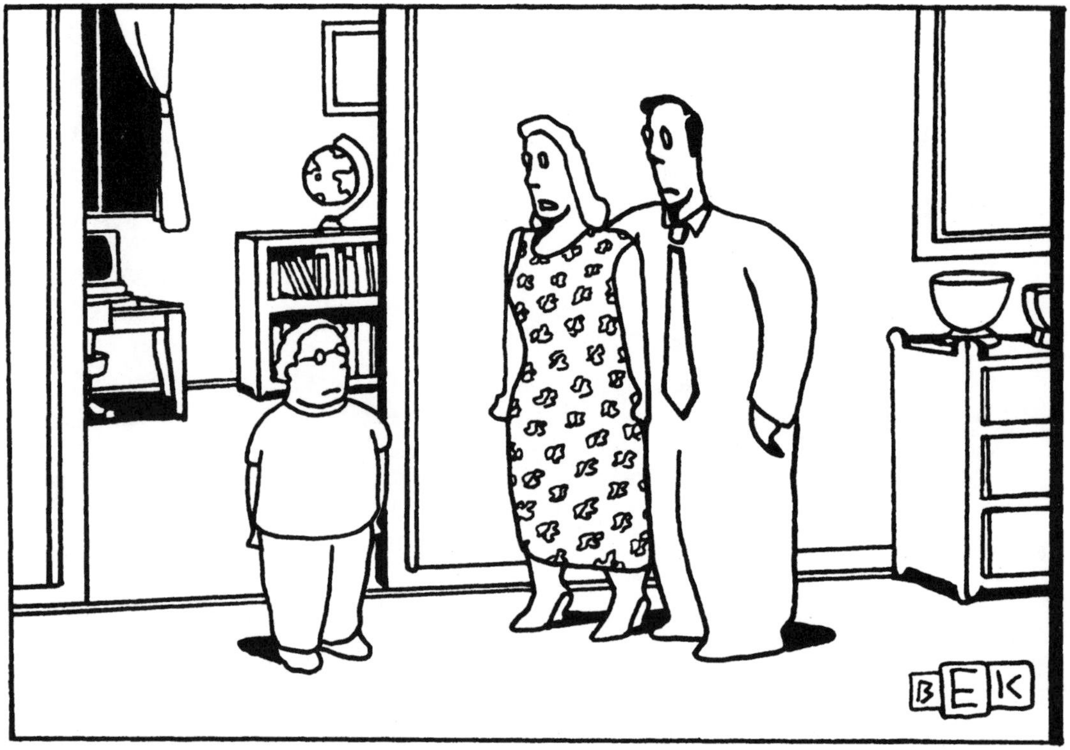
BEK

*"We're neither software nor hardware. We're your parents."*

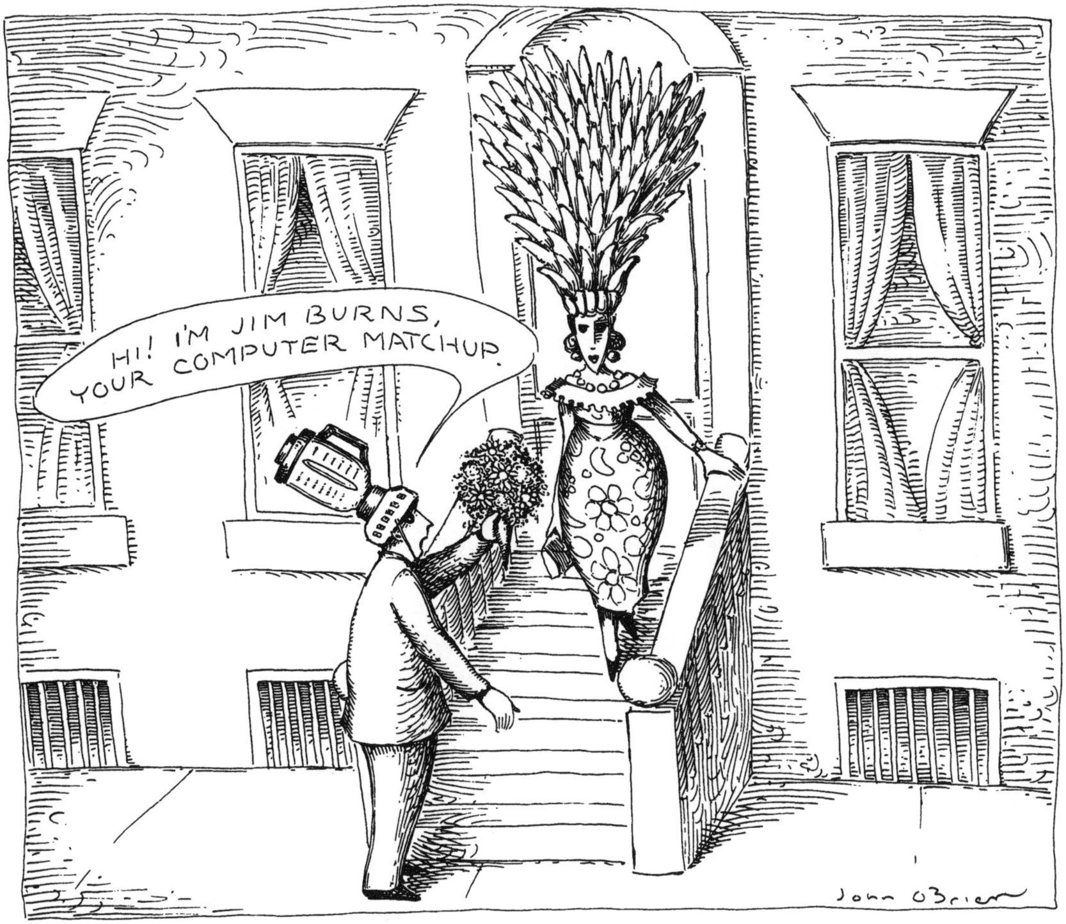
HI! I'M JIM BURNS, YOUR COMPUTER MATCHUP.
John O'Brien

"When we implant your pacemaker, we can, for a modest additional fee, also implant your beeper."

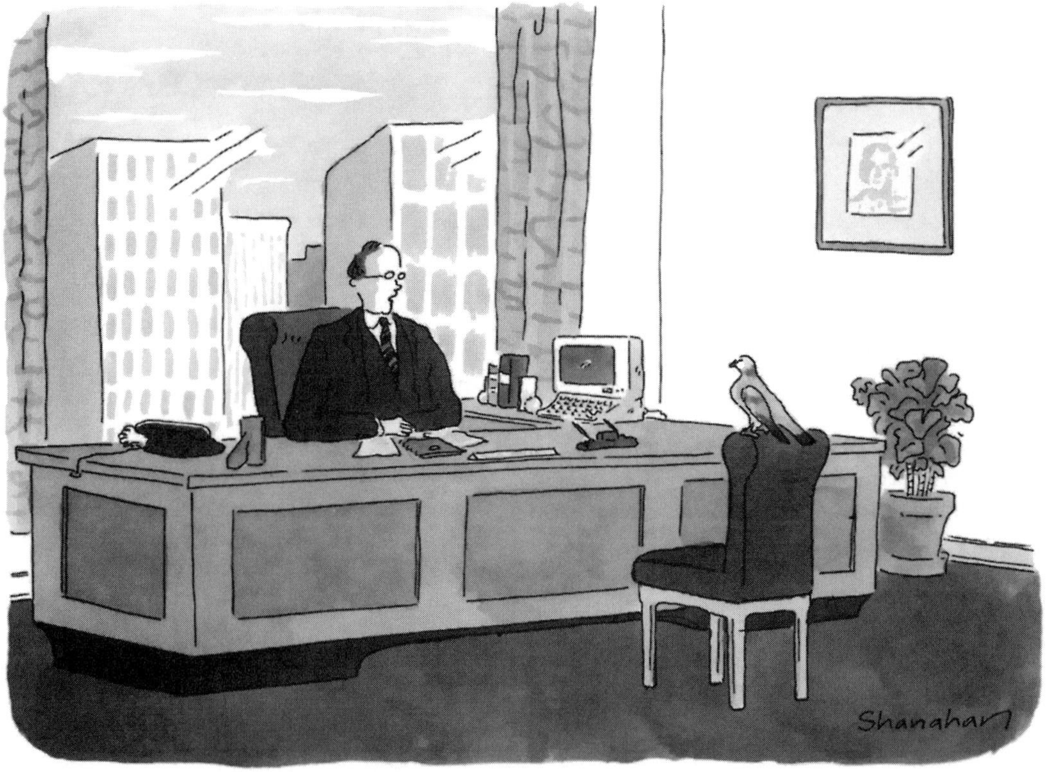
Shanahan

*"Thank you very much, but I'm more than satisfied with my present long-distance carrier."*

MORE MORE MORE MORE MORE
MORE
MORE
MORE
MORE
MORE
MORE
MORE
MORE
MORE
MORE
MORE
MORE
MORE
MORE
MORE
MORE
← MORE
MORE
MORE MORE MORE MORE
MORE MORE MORE MORE
MORE MORE MORE MORE
MORE
MORE/MORE
MORE MORE MORE MORE
MORE
MORE
MORE
MORE
cheney

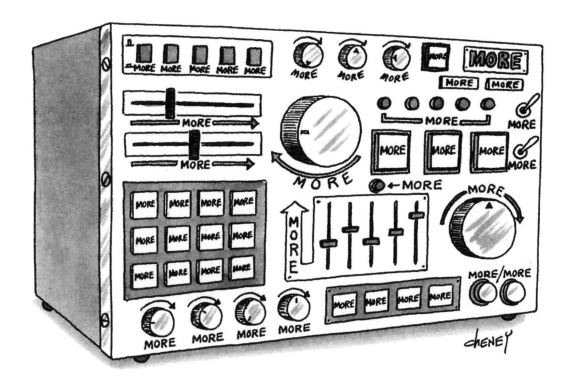

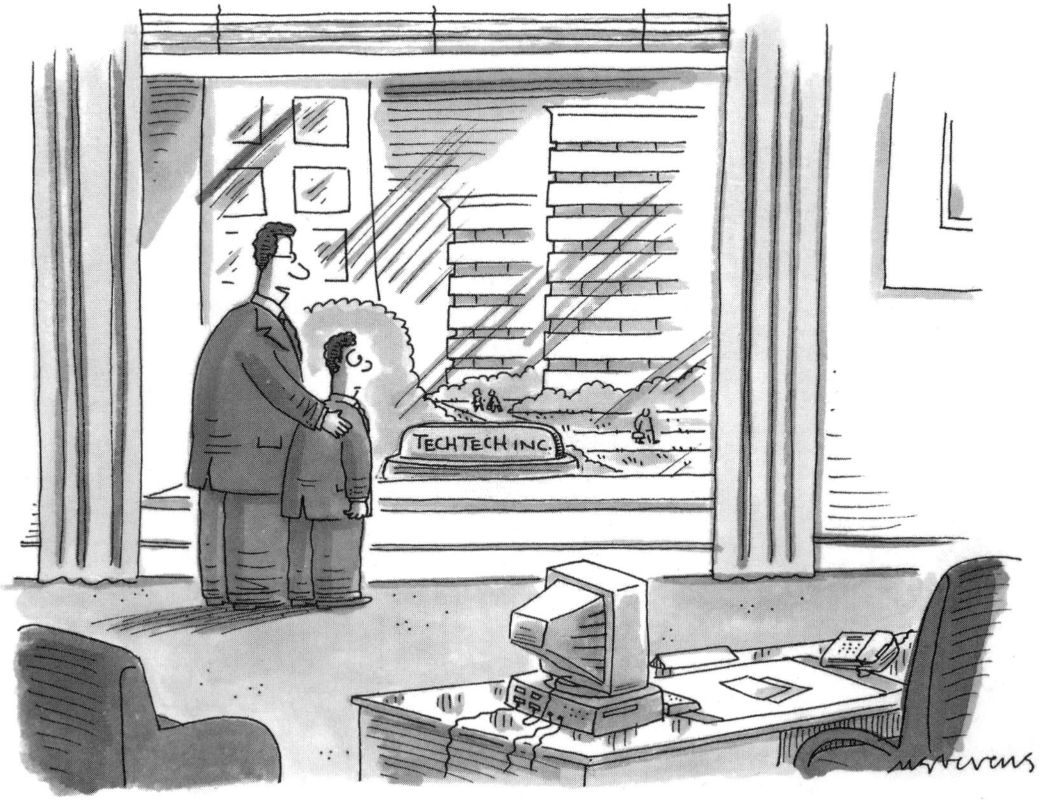
TECHTECH INC.

*"Someday, son, all this will belong to Bill Gates."*

*"What about that! His brain still uses the old vacuum tubes."*

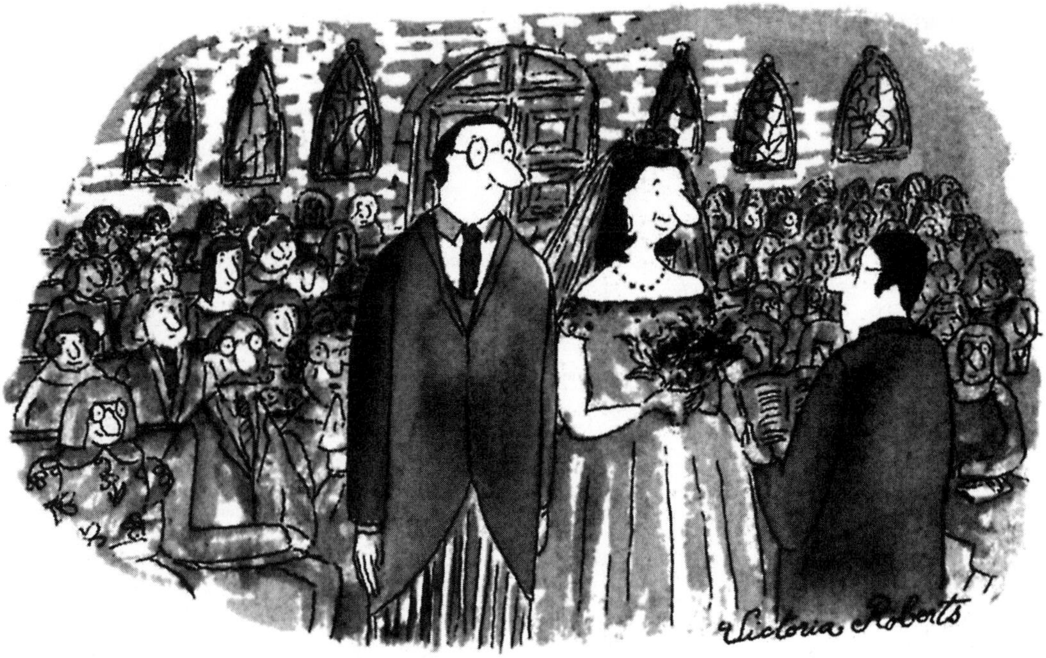
Victoria Roberts

*"I'm delighted to love, honor, and obey, but I'm keeping my electronic rights."*

"*You say you love me, but I'm not on your speed dial.*"

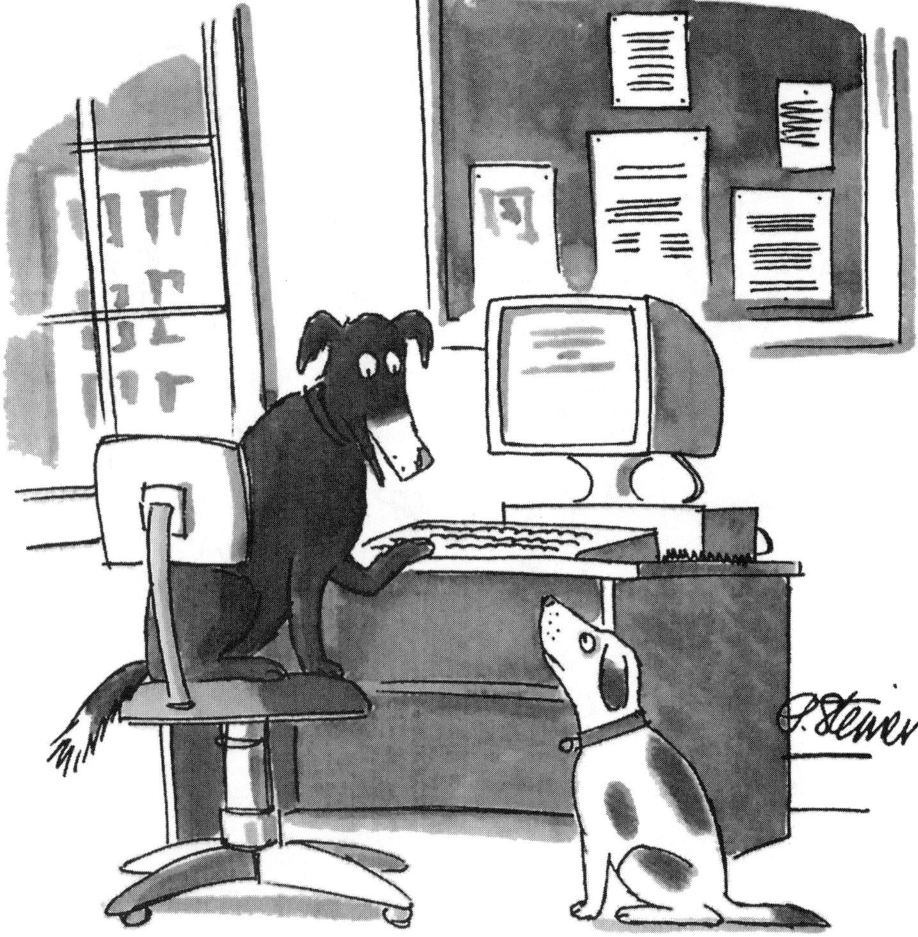
P. Steiner

*"On the Internet, nobody knows you're a dog."*

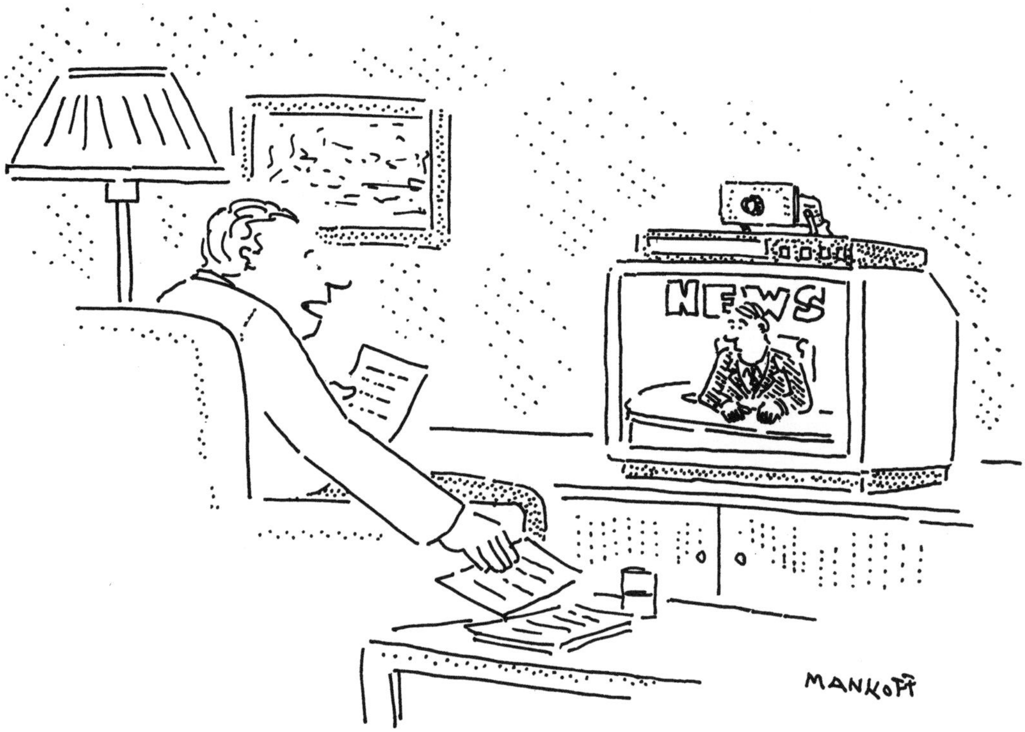
NEWS
MANKOFF

*"The much ballyhooed era of TV interactivity took a step closer to reality today."*

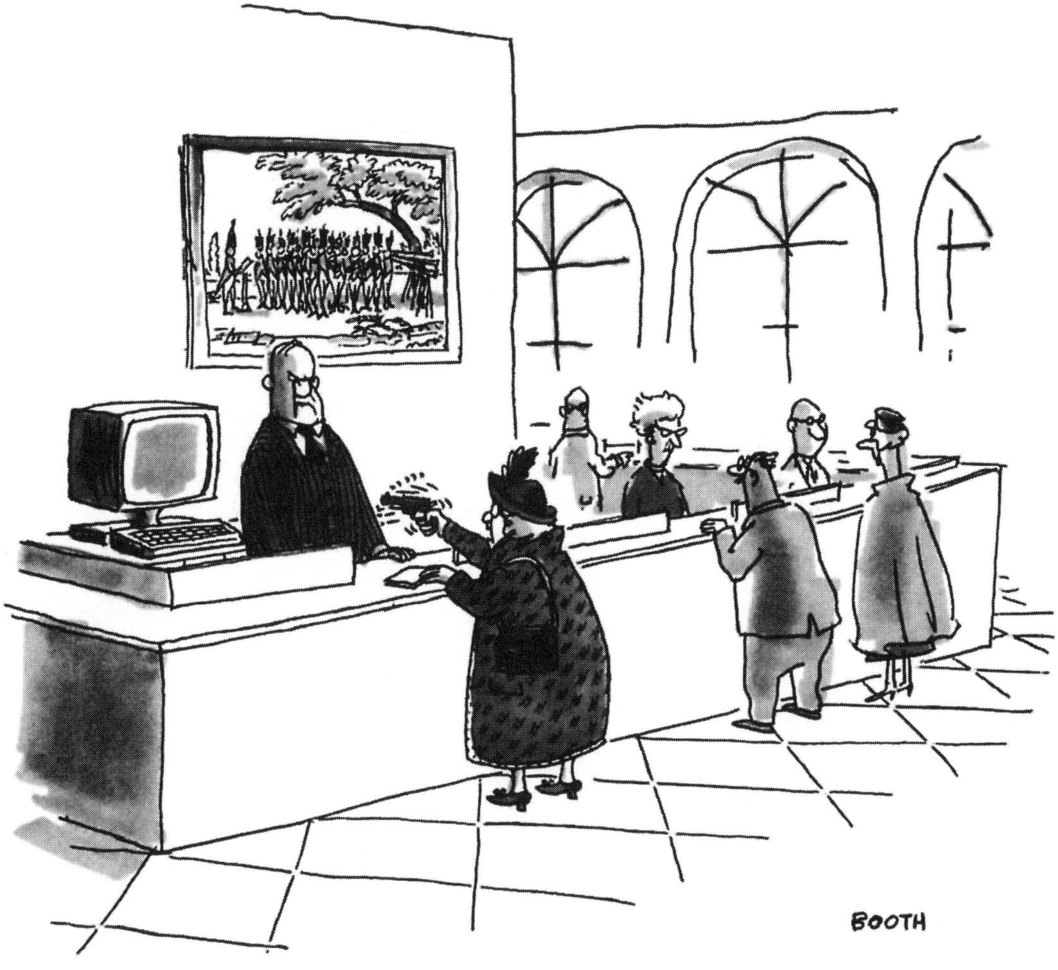
BOOTH

*"Stand aside, Gruenwald! It's the computer I'm blowing away!"*

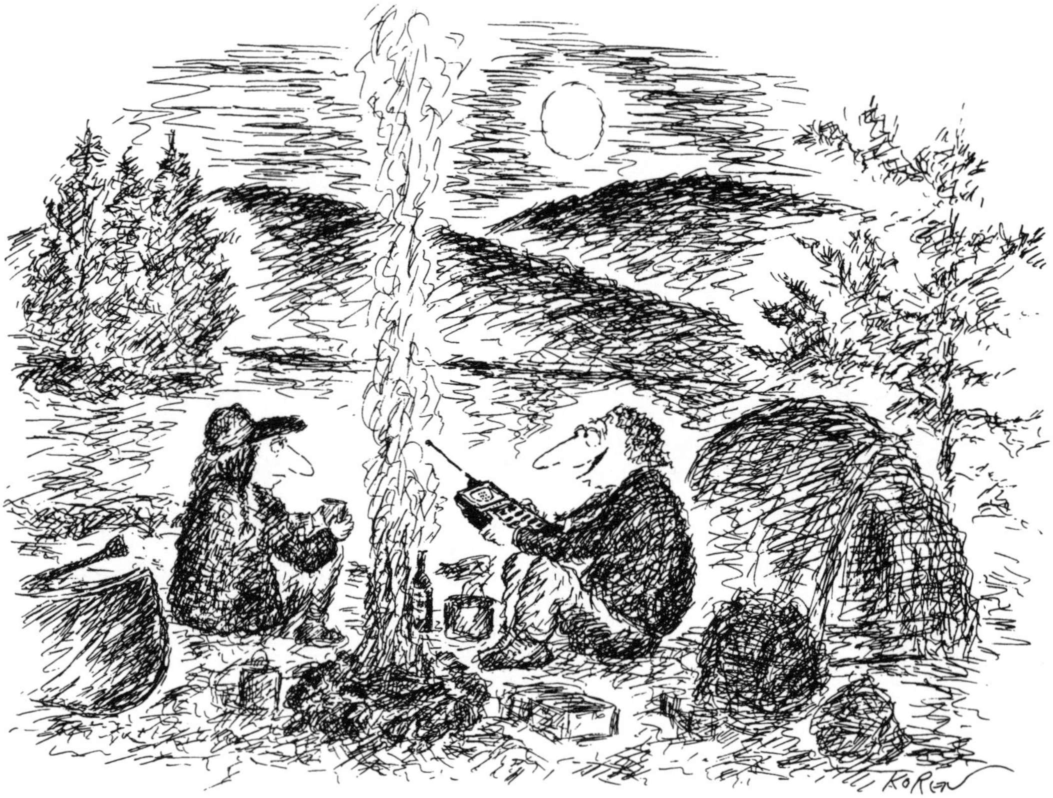
KOREN

*"Who can we call?"*

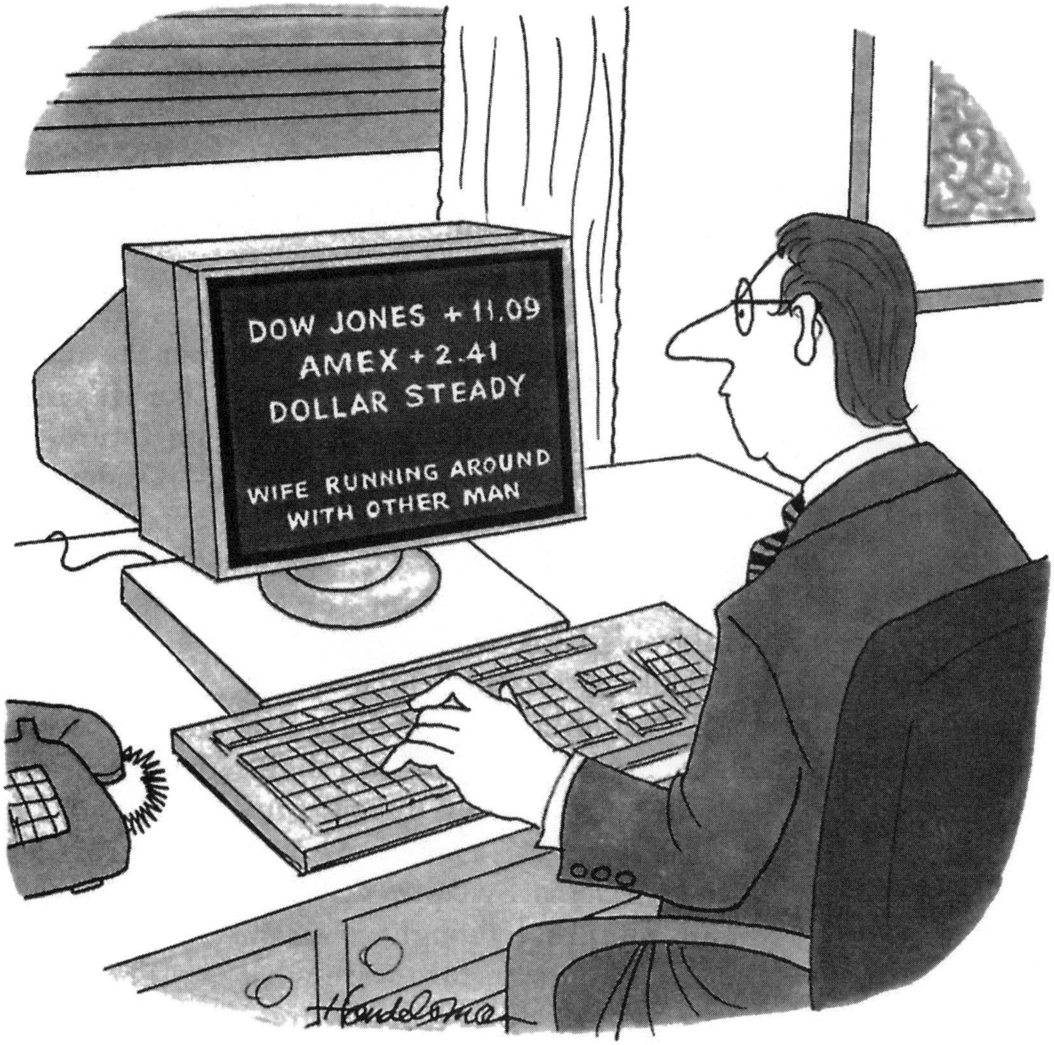
DOW JONES + 11.09
AMEX + 2.41
DOLLAR STEADY
WIFE RUNNING AROUND
WITH OTHER MAN

"We can pause, Stu—we can even try fast-forwarding—
but we can never rewind."

MOM'S
ELECTRONICS
WE HAVE
COMPUTERS-
IF YOU'RE SURE THAT'S WHAT YOU WANT
ANSWERING MACHINES
YOU'RE NOT FOOLING ANYBODY-
I KNOW YOU'RE THERE
YES, WE CARRY CD PLAYERS, SINCE NOW YOUR OLD STEREO JUST ISN'T GOOD ENOUGH. IS IT?
FAX
EQUIPMENT
FOR BIG SHOTS IN A BIG HURRY
CELLULAR PHONES
GO AHEAD, GIVE YOURSELF A BRAIN TUMOR
R. Chast

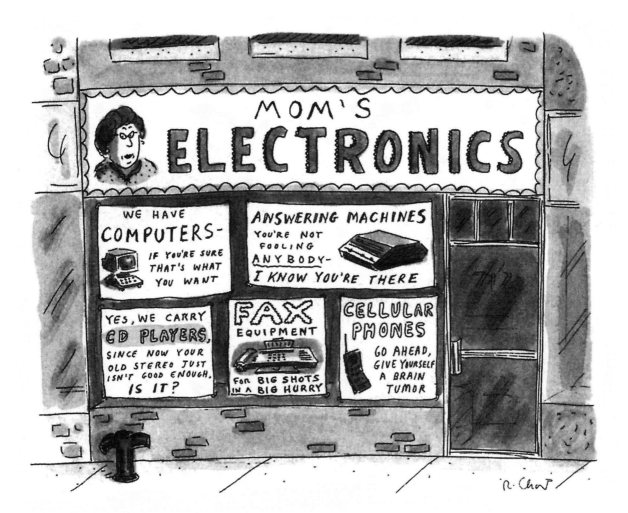

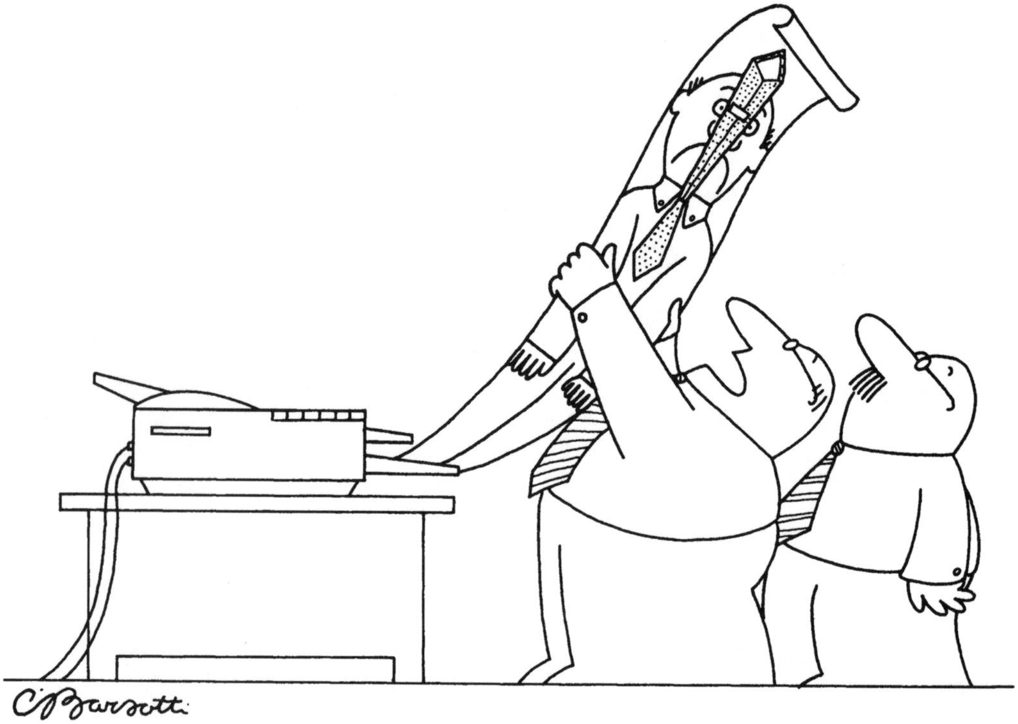
C Barsotti

*"My God, there's been a terrible accident in our Chicago office!"*

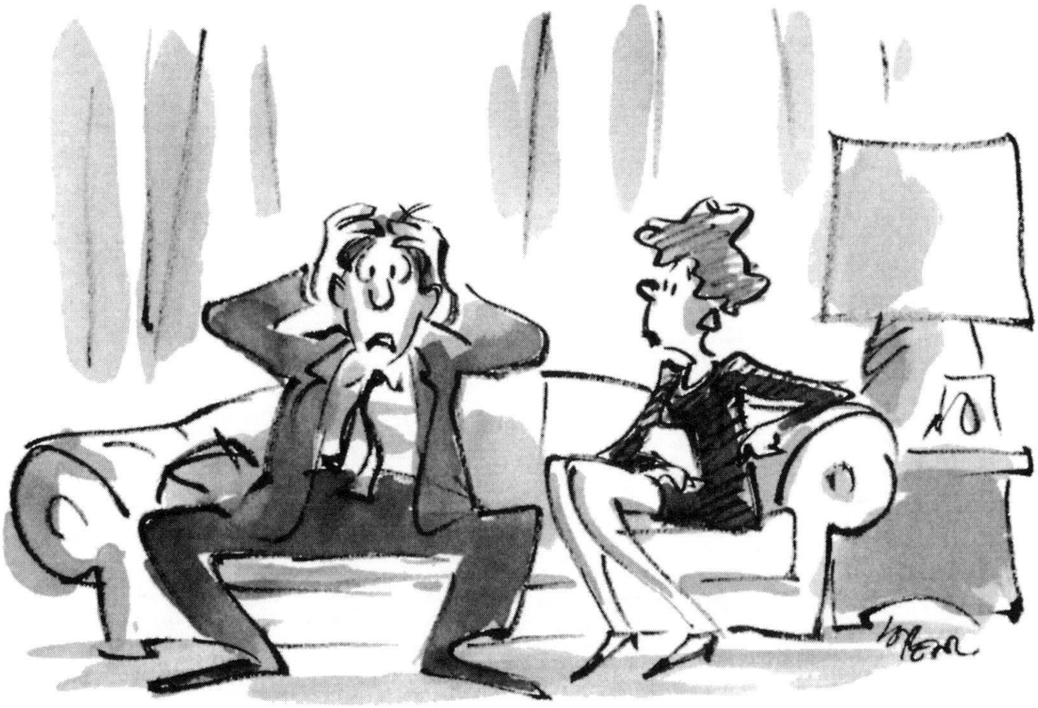
LORENZ

*"Forgive me, Doris, but some computer hacker from Roslyn, Long Island, has just gained access to my feelings."*

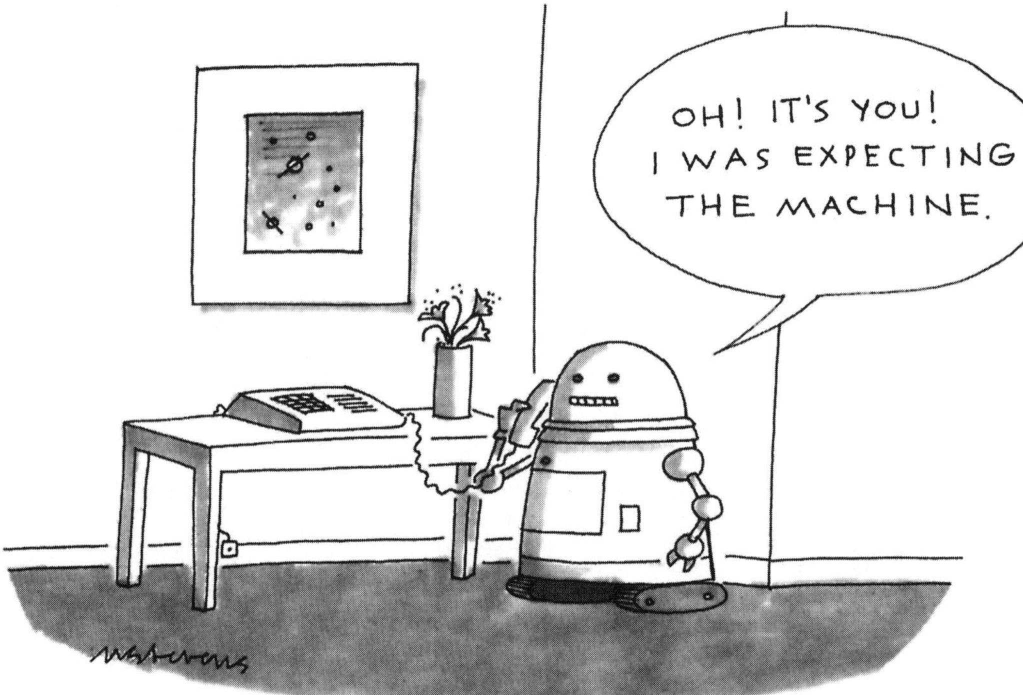
OH! IT'S YOU! I WAS EXPECTING THE MACHINE.

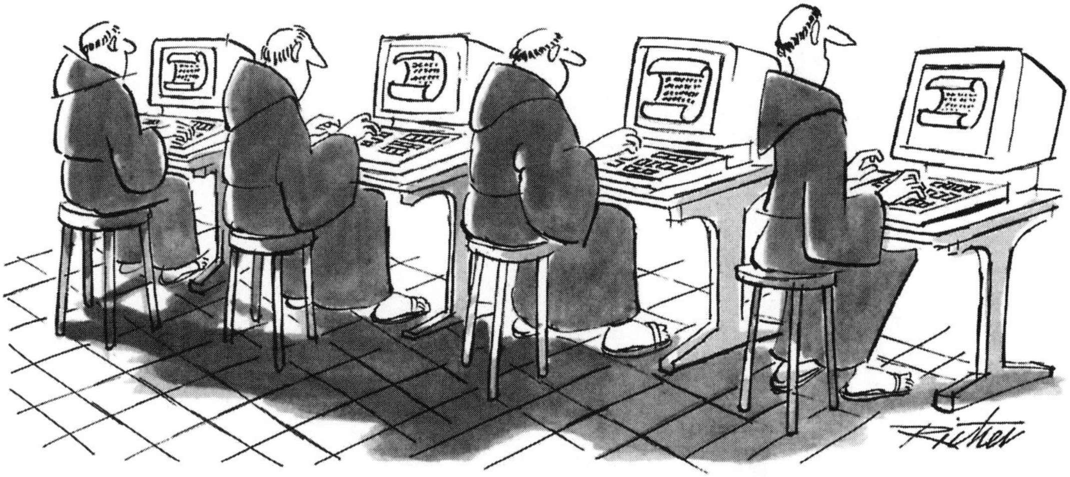
Richter

*"Do we tip it?"*

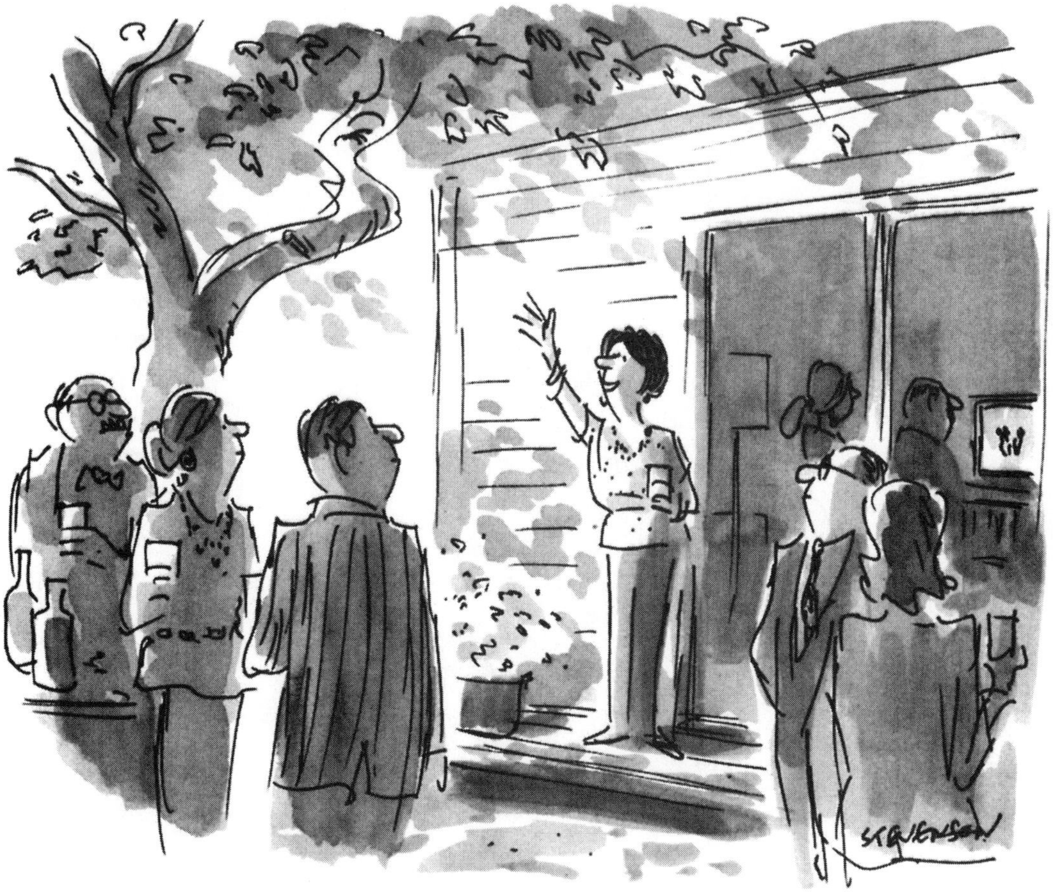
STEVENSON

*"Everybody in! We have videotapes of the first hour of the party!"*

MAINFRAME    LAPTOP    POCKET

THE COMPLETE CYCLE
WASH
FILL TUB
RINSE
START
SPIN
LOSE SOCK
R. Chast

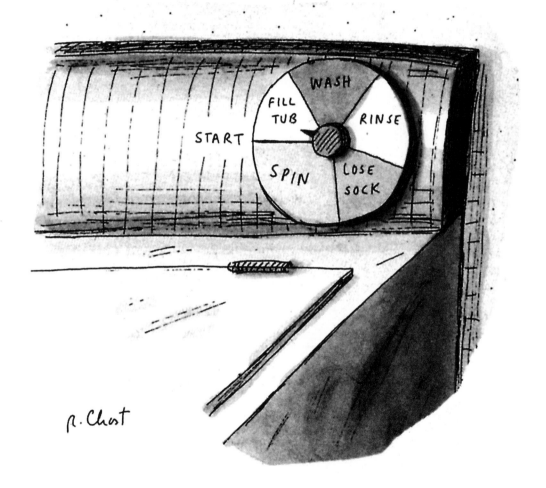

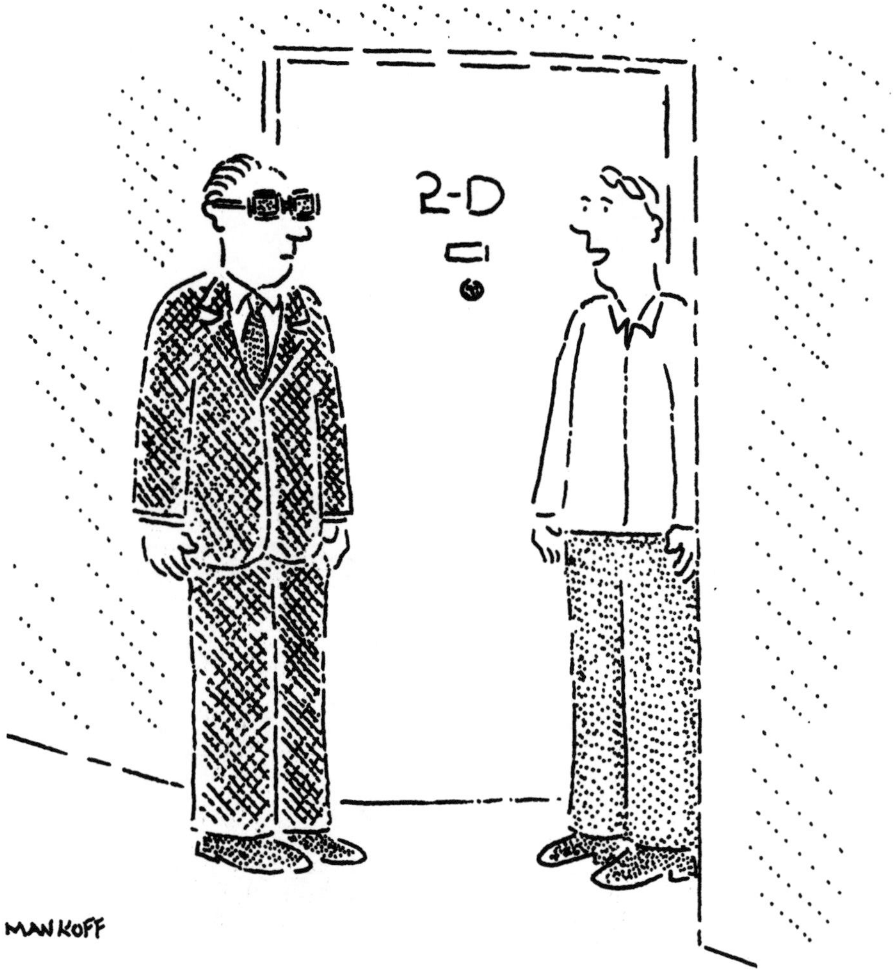
2-D
MANKOFF

*"I think you're looking for 3-D."*

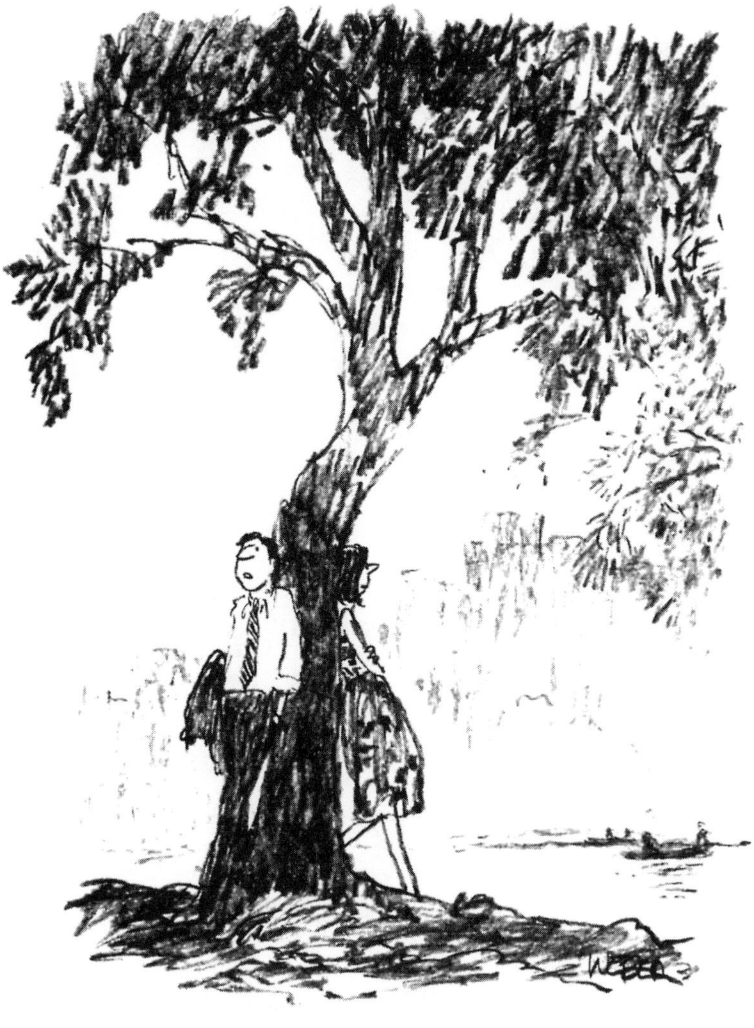
WEBER

*"Already my computer is outmoded, but I try to tell myself that my computer isn't me."*

"Sometimes I ask myself, 'Where will it ever end?'"

"*Dennis, I would like to talk to you for a minute—off-line.*"

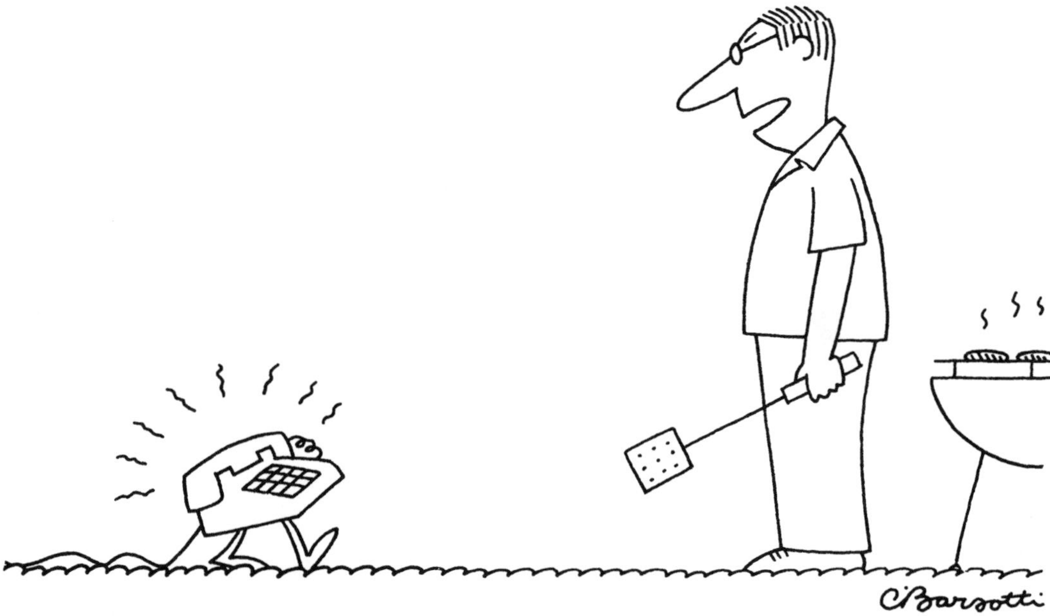
CBarsotti

*"What the hell sort of convenient new feature is this?"*

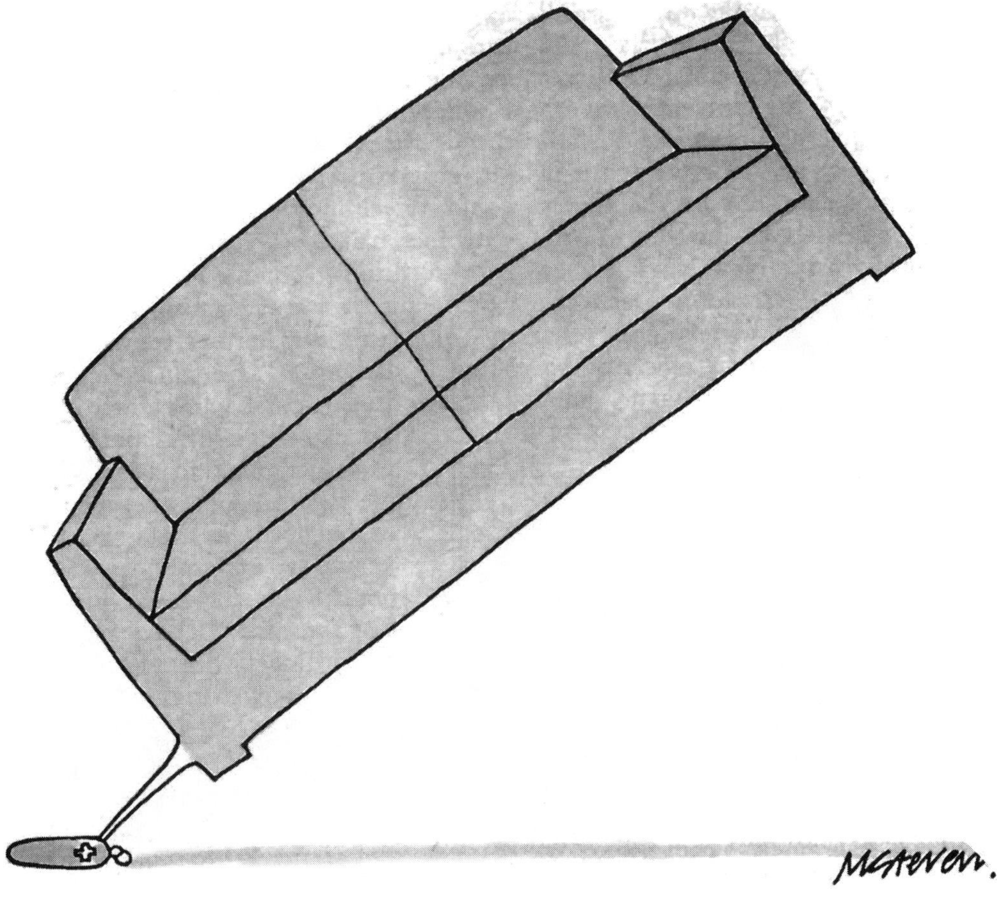
McSteven.

SWISS ARMY COUCH

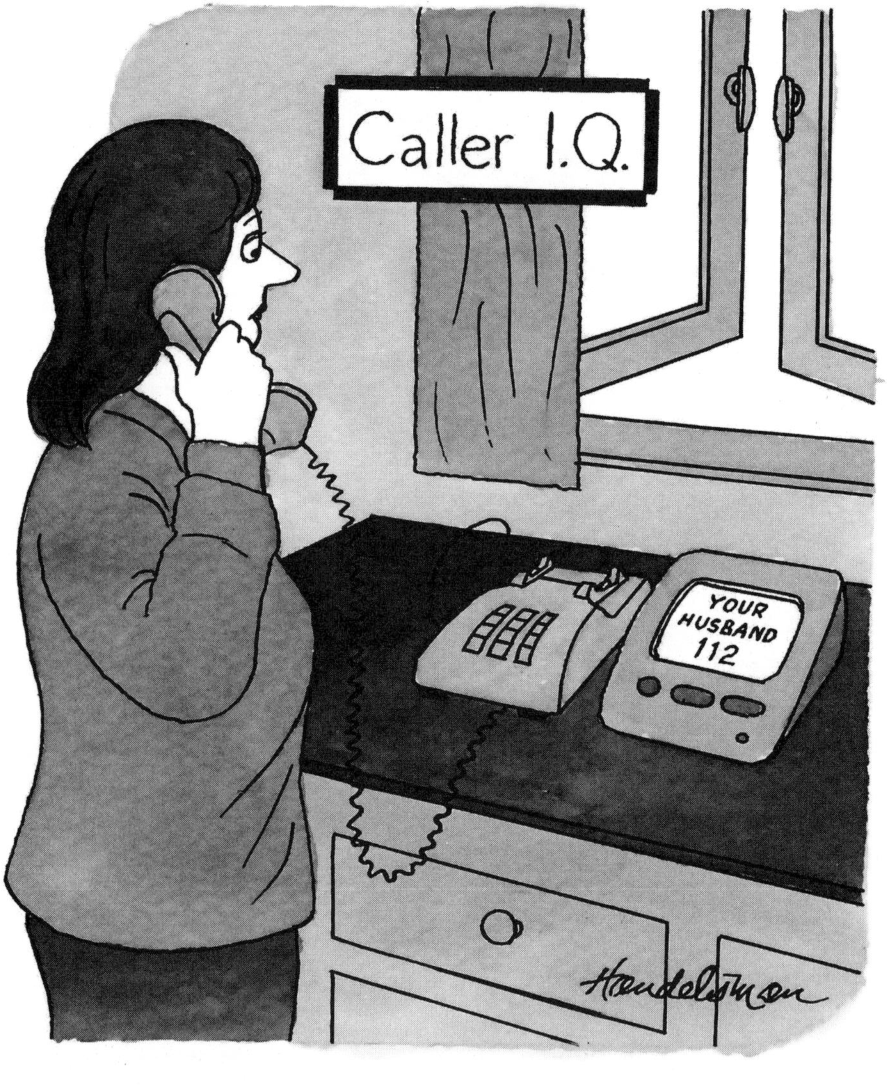
Caller I.Q.
YOUR HUSBAND
112
Handelsman

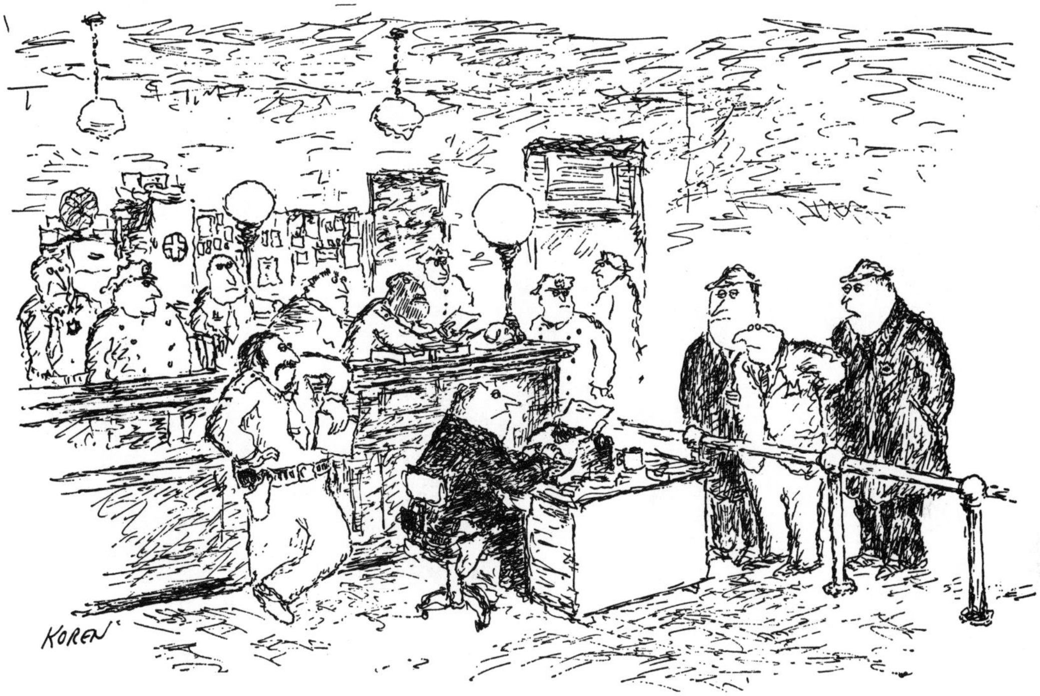
KOREN

*"He's charged with expressing contempt for data-processing."*

*"I just realized, Howard, that everything in this apartment is more sophisticated than we are."*

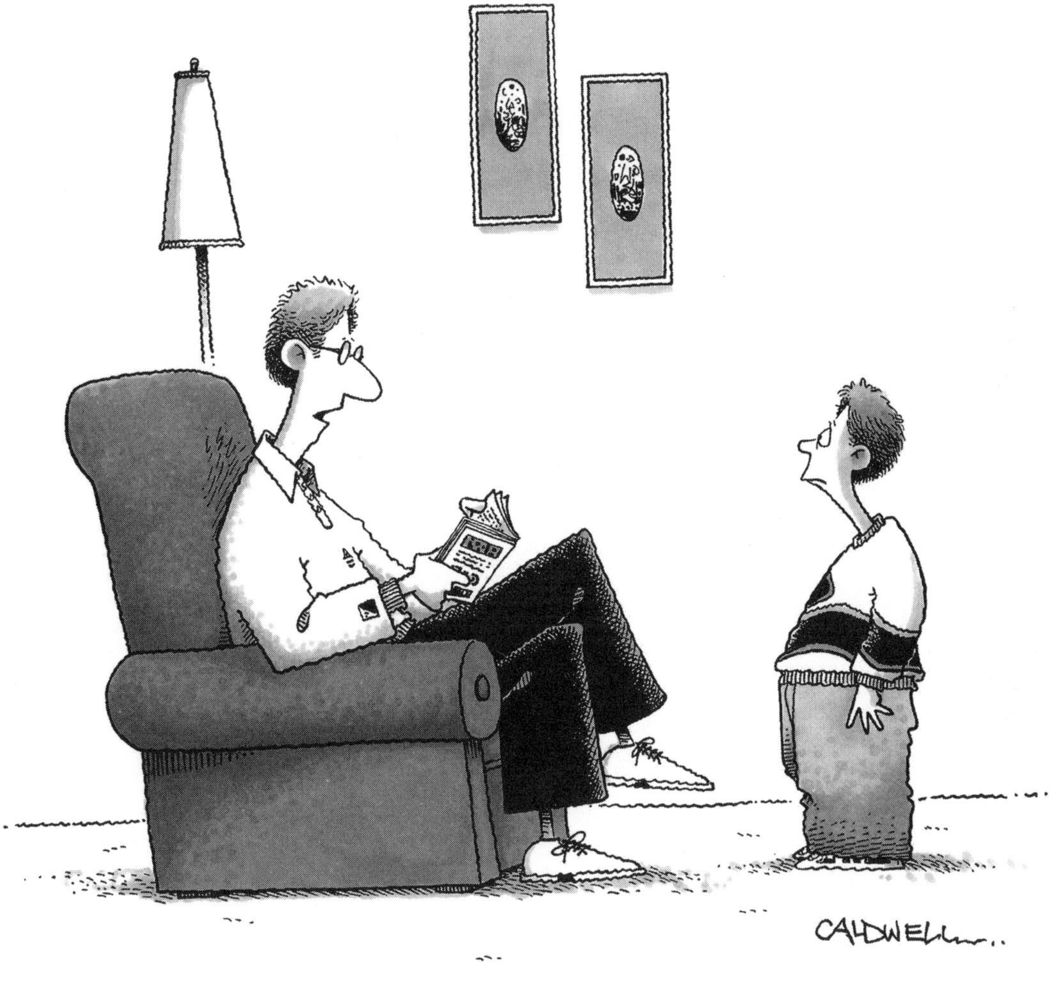
CALDWELL

*"Go ask your search engine."*

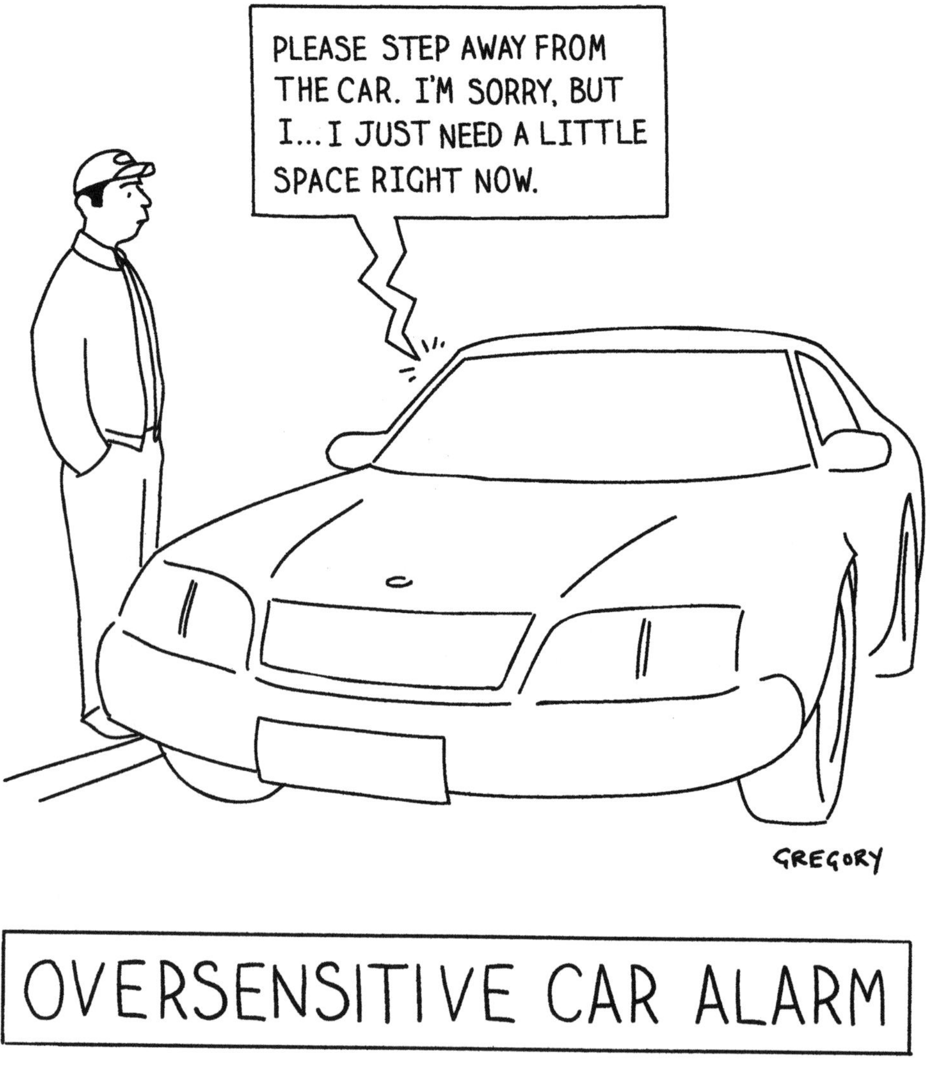
PLEASE STEP AWAY FROM THE CAR. I'M SORRY, BUT I... I JUST NEED A LITTLE SPACE RIGHT NOW.
GREGORY

OVERSENSITIVE CAR ALARM

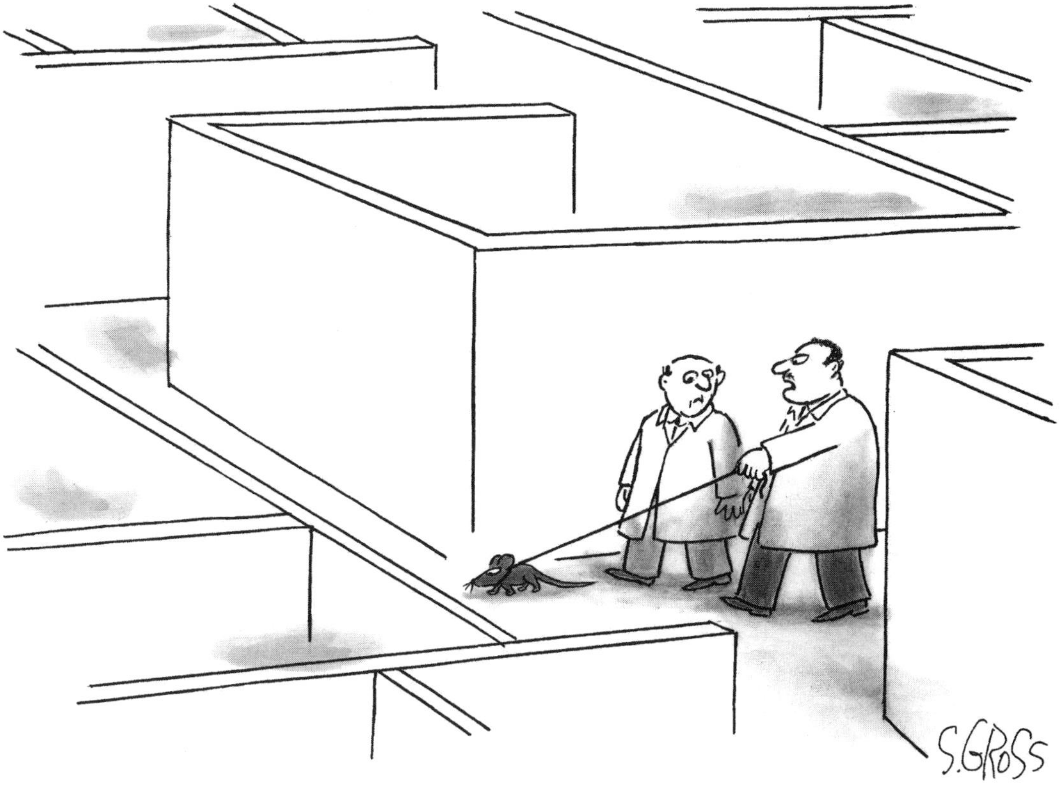
S.GROSS

*"Genetic engineering got us into this mess, and genetic engineering will get us out of it."*

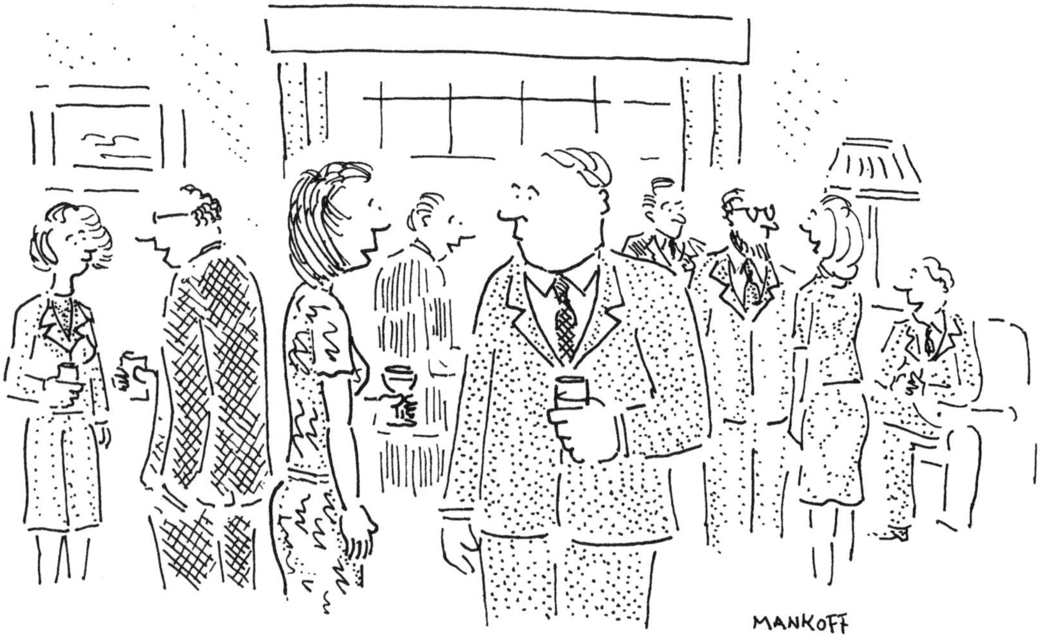
MANKOFF

*"I haven't read it yet, but I've downloaded it from the Internet."*

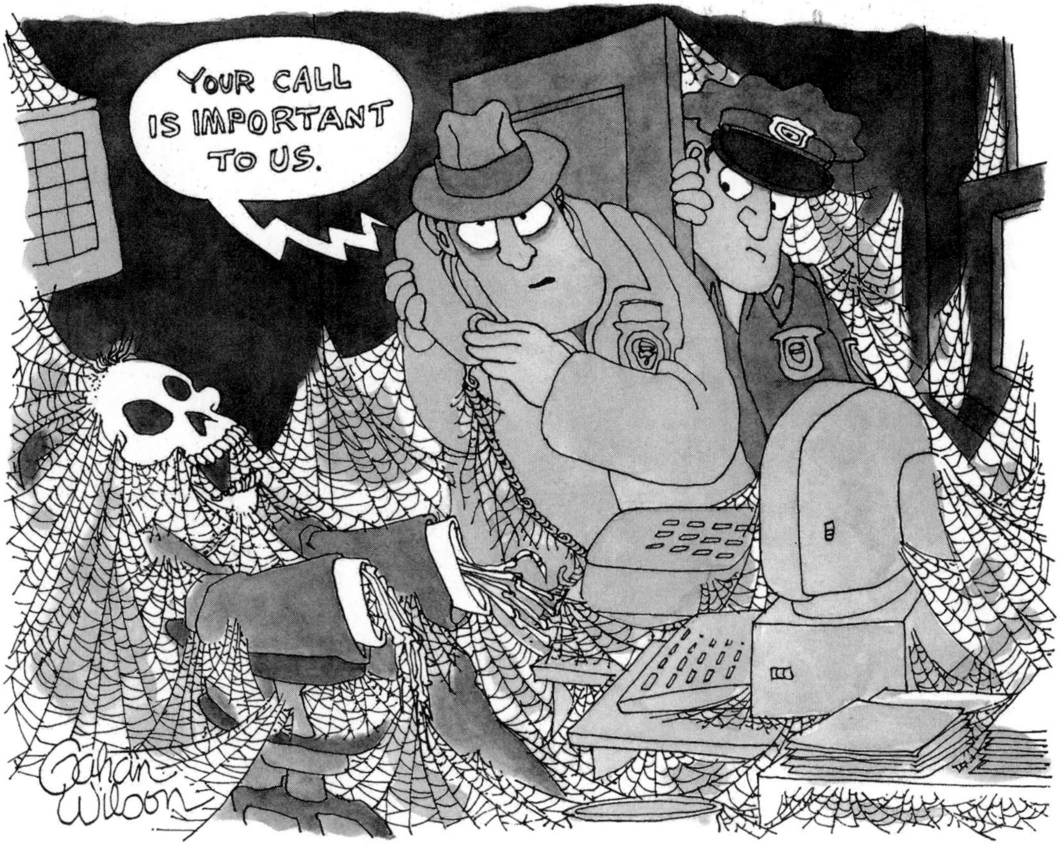
YOUR CALL IS IMPORTANT TO US.

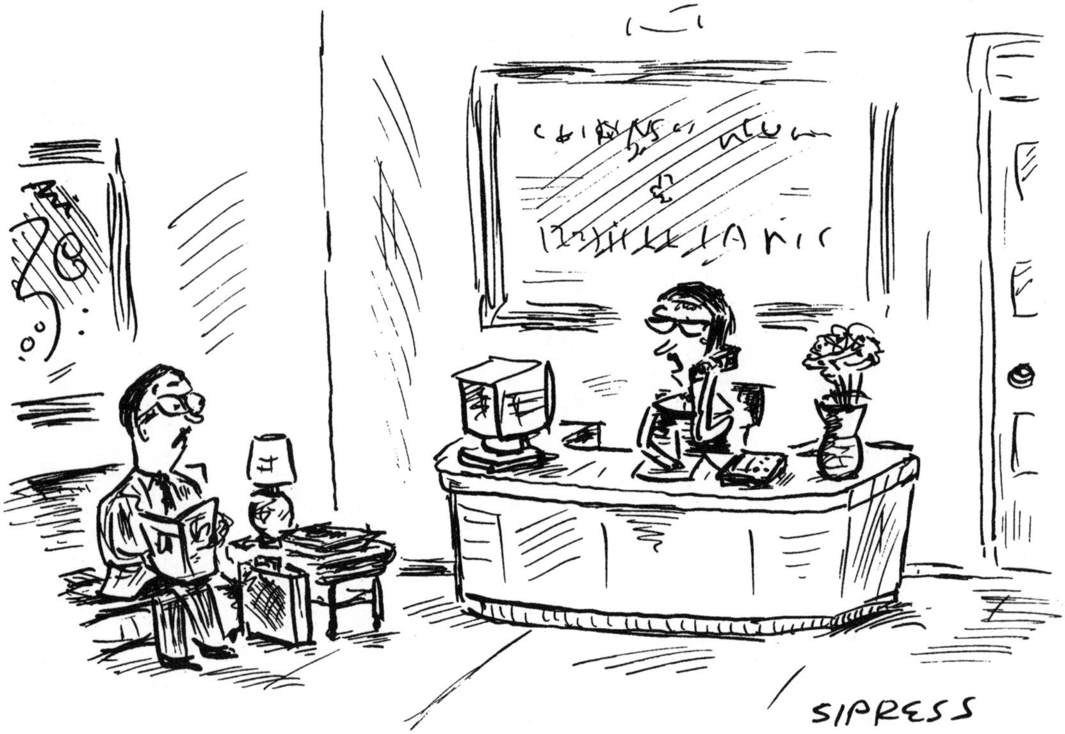
SIPRESS

*"He's dead. Would you like his voice mail?"*

"You will never catch up with the new technology."

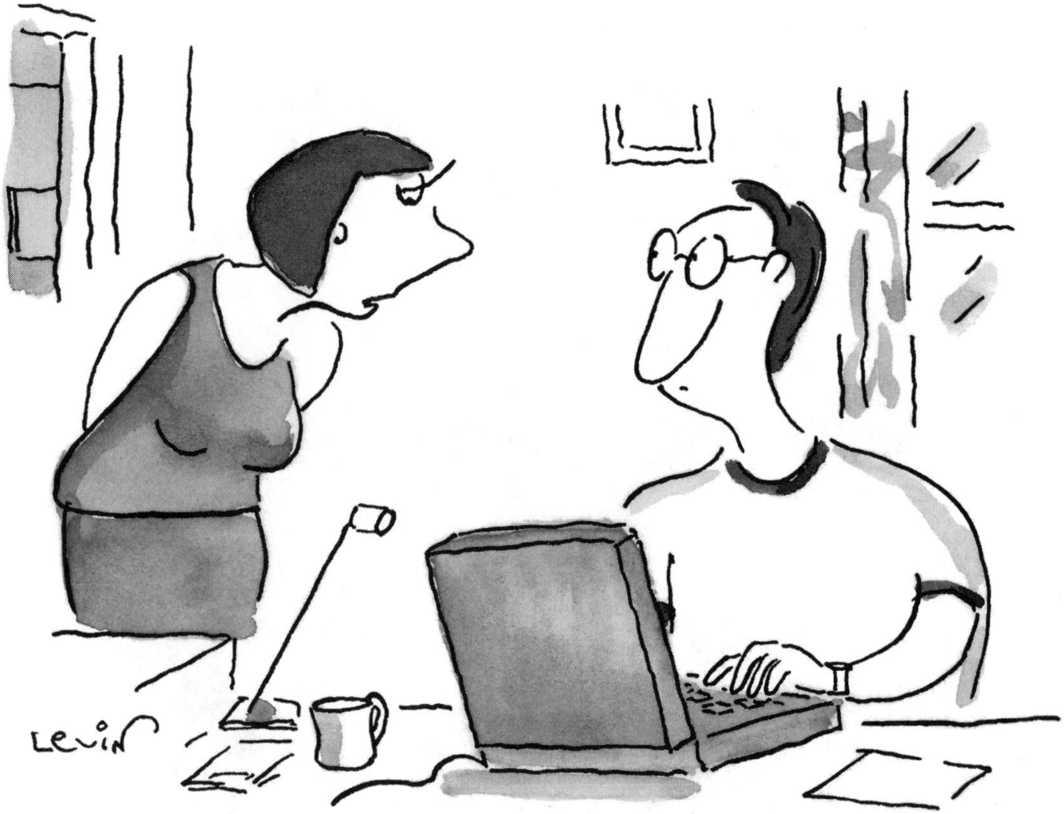
LEVIN

*"And just what was that little window you clicked off when I came in?"*

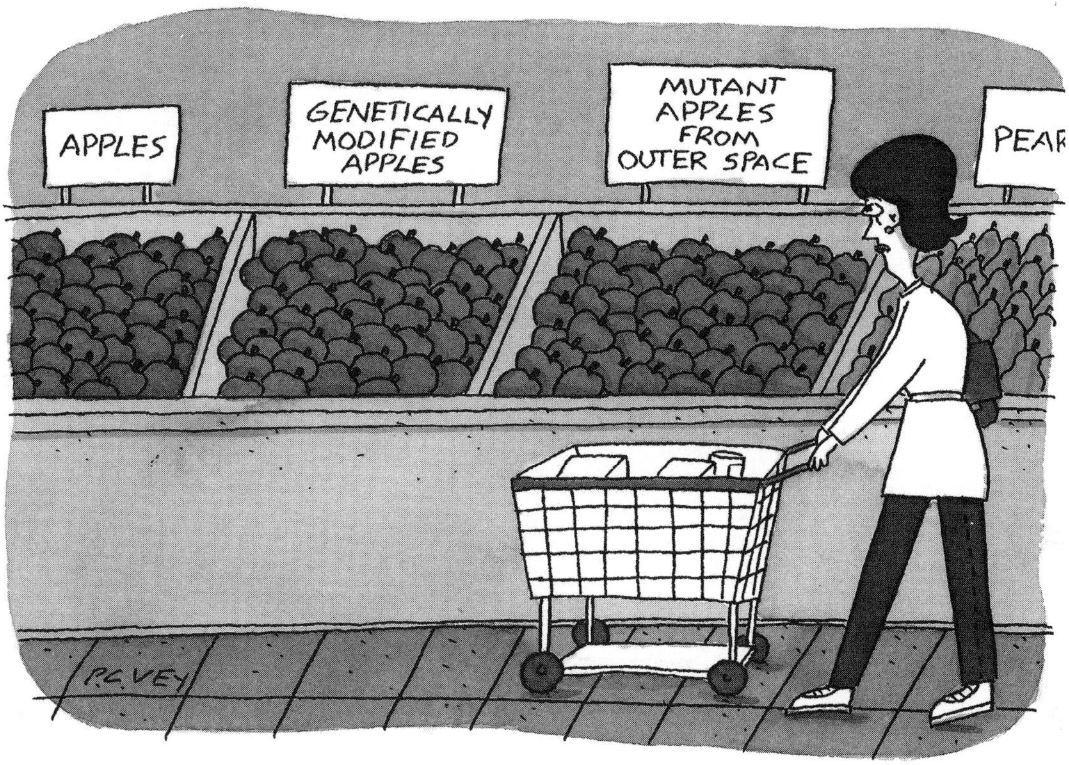
APPLES
GENETICALLY MODIFIED APPLES
MUTANT APPLES FROM OUTER SPACE
PEAR
P.C.VEY

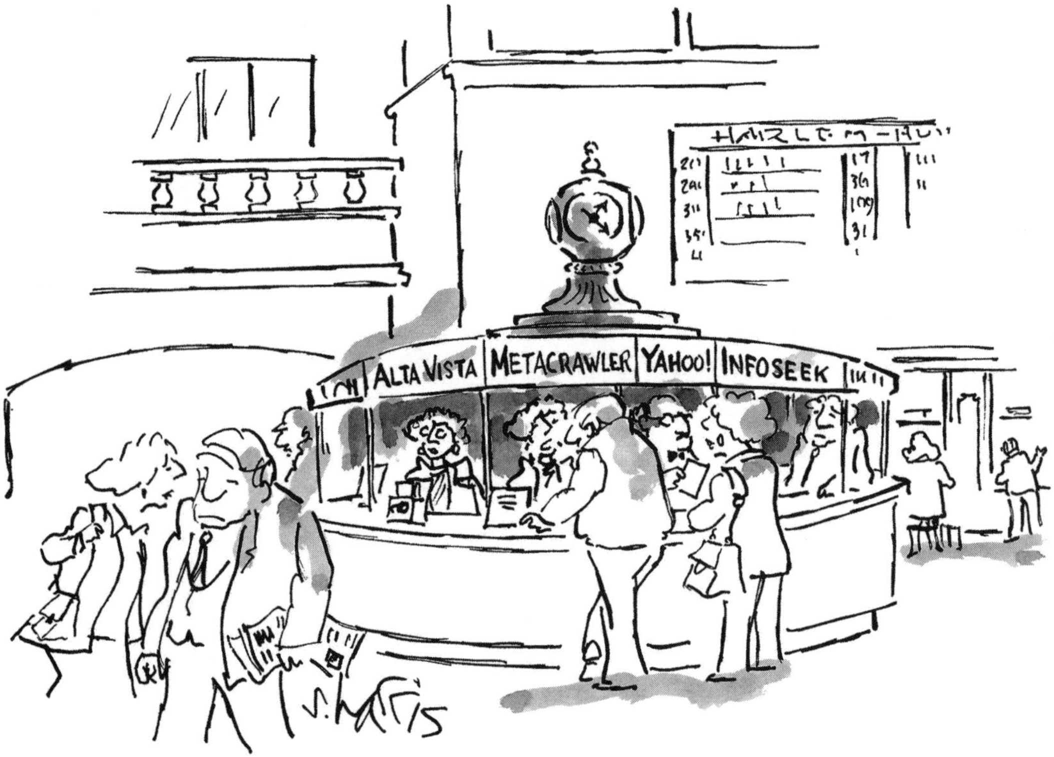
ALTA VISTA
METACRAWLER
YAHOO!
INFOSEEK
S. HARRIS

# CASH MACHINES from ACROSS THE LAND

The Big Purse
East Lubbock, New Jersey

Dad's Pocket Casheteria
Twelve Buckets, Nebraska

The Weeping Bankbook
Hensteeth, Alabama

Mattress o' Moola
Knorl, Idaho

R. Chrst

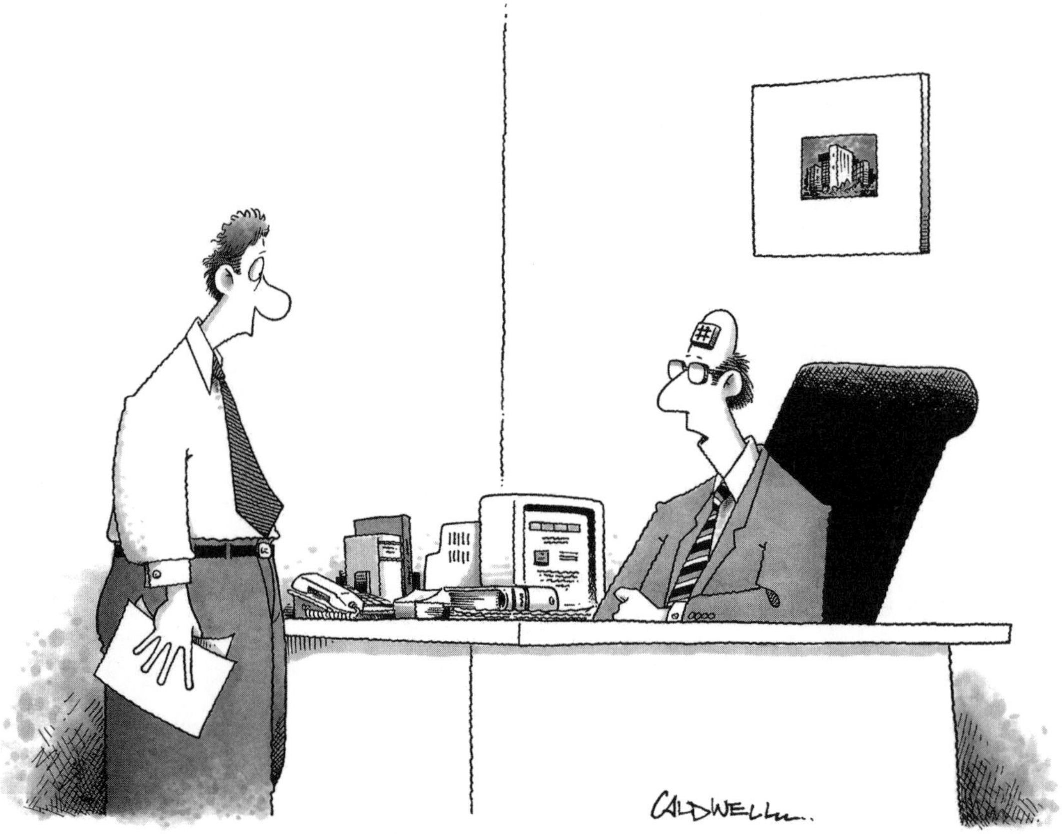
CALDWELL

*"If you require immediate assistance, press the pound sign."*

"No, the computers are up. We're down."

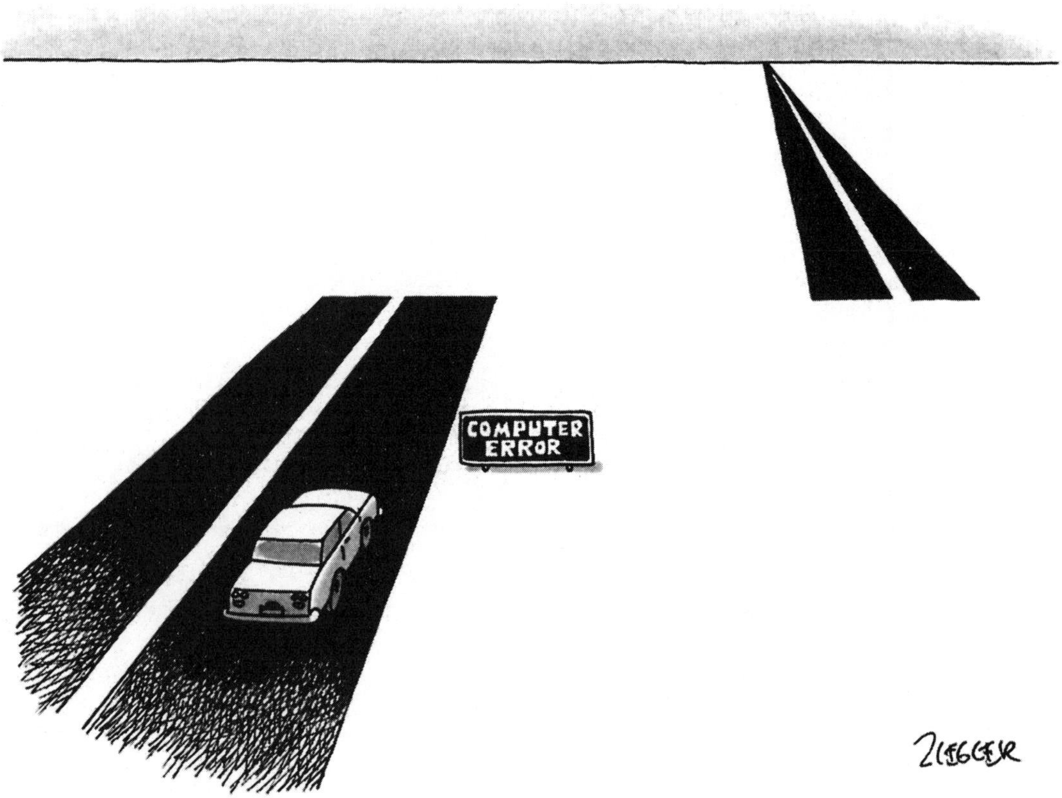
COMPUTER
ERROR
ZIEGLER

"I only draw with software."

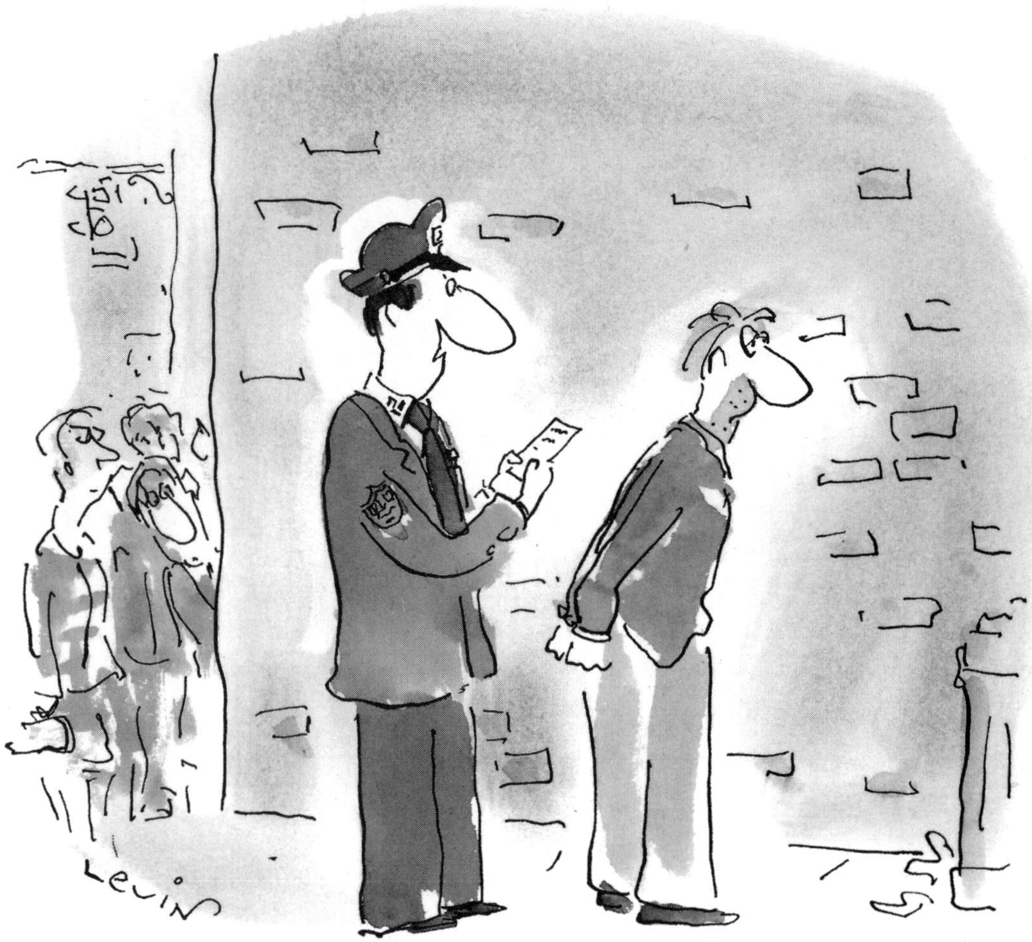
LEVIN

*"You have the right to remain silent. Anything you say may be used against you in a court of law, newspapers, periodicals, radio, television, all electronic media, and technologies yet to be invented."*

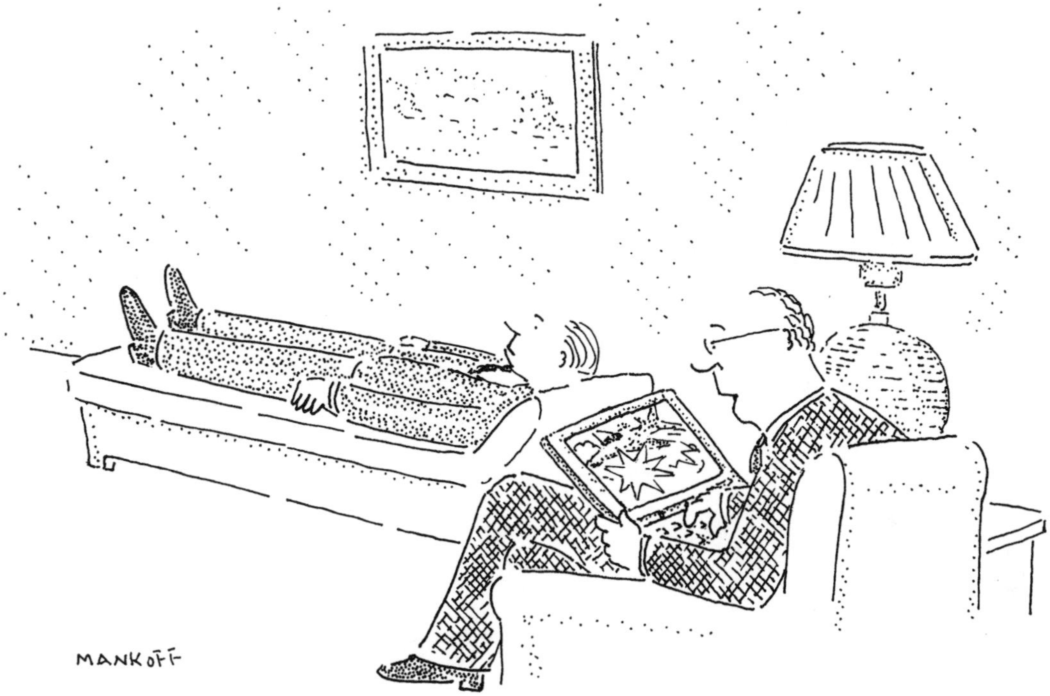
MANKOFF

*"You think you have problems? My entire wing command was just destroyed."*

*"Big Tony's Web site—get rid of it."*

# INDEX OF ARTISTS

Marisa Acocella, 27

Charles Addams, 86

Charles Barsotti, 5, 76, 88

George Booth, 35, 71

John Caldwell, 32, 93, 104

Roz Chast, 7, 19, 50, 75, 83, 103

Tom Cheney, 1, 14, 63

Richard Cline, 44, 67

Frank Cotham, 13, 40, 65

Michael Crawford, 52

Leo Cullum, 4, 22, 60

J.C. Duffy, 45

Ed Fisher, 33

Mort Gerberg, 29, 87

Alex Gregory, 31, 94

Sam Gross, 37, 95

William Haefeli, 34

William Hamilton, 20

J.B. Handelsman, 17, 38, 55, 73, 90

Sidney Harris, 56, 102

Bruce Eric Kaplan, 58

Edward Koren, 36, 72, 91

Arnie Levin, 3, 25, 42, 46, 100, 108

Lee Lorenz, 28, 48, 61, 77, 92

Robert Mankoff, 21, 51, 70, 84, 96, 109

Michael Maslin, 16, 74

Warren Miller, 30, 105

John O'Brien, 59

Donald Reilly, 53, 107

Mischa Richter, 24, 79

Victoria Roberts, 43, 66

Al Ross, 18

Bernard Schoenbaum, 8, 80

Danny Shanahan, 41, 62

David Sipress, 9, 98

Barbara Smaller, 10

Peter Steiner, 47, 68, 110

Mick Stevens, 12, 23, 39, 64, 78, 89

James Stevenson, 81

Mike Twohy, 6

P.C. Vey, 15, 101

Dean Vietor, 54

Robert Weber, 11, 85, 99

Gahan Wilson, 57, 97

Jack Ziegler, 2, 26, 49, 69, 82, 106

*The New Yorker Book of Technology Cartoons CD-ROM*

This is a legal agreement between you and Bloomberg L.P. ("Bloomberg"). By installing, copying, or otherwise using this CD-ROM, you agree to be bound by the terms and conditions of this Agreement. If, at any time, you do not wish to accept the terms and conditions of this Agreement, you may not use the CD-ROM. Bloomberg reserves the right to change the terms of this Agreement and/or withdraw permission to use the CD-ROM at any time and for any reason.

You acquire no title, rights, or licenses in or to the content made available by Bloomberg other than the limited right to use the content in accordance with this Agreement. As between you and Bloomberg, Bloomberg retains all intellectual property and other rights to this content in all jurisdictions and provides it to you solely for your personal, non-commercial use and not for professional use or publication. Bloomberg does not: (a) make any warranty, express or implied, with respect to the use of the content and software, including without limitation that the CD-ROM is compatible with your equipment or free of errors or viruses, worms or "Trojan horses", as provides the content "AS IS"; (b) guarantee the accuracy, completeness, usefulness or adequacy of the content and software; or (c) make any endorsement, express or implied, of the content and software. Bloomberg, its suppliers, and third-party agents shall have no liability for any errors in the content or for lost profits, losses or direct, incidental, consequential, special or punitive damages in connection with the furnishing, performance, or use of such content. This Agreement shall be governed and construed in accordance with the laws of the United States and the State of New York, without giving effect to conflicts-of-law principles thereof. You agree to submit to the personal jurisdiction of the state and federal courts located in New York County in the State of New York with respect to any legal proceedings that may arise in connection with the CD-ROM or from a dispute as to the interpretation or breach of this Agreement.

All the cartoons are © copyrighted by The New Yorker and CARTOONBANK.COM. You may not use Bloomberg's trademarks, trade names or service marks in any manner which creates the impression that such names and marks belong to or are associated with you or are used with Bloomberg's consent, and you acknowledge that you have no ownership rights in and to any of these names and marks.

---

*Instructions for using your CD-ROM to e-mail cartoons:*

1) Insert CD-ROM into your computer (PC or MAC). Note: It won't work at all well in audio CD players.
2) Open your e-mail program and enter the address(es) to which you want to send cartoons.
3) Say anything witty or warm you wish to impart to the addressee(s).
4) Using the attachment function in your e-mail program, find and open the CD-ROM on your desktop. Refer to your e-mail program's instructions for sending attachments.

NOTE: All cartoons are numbered by the page number in the book (that is, 001 is page 1, 101 is page 101, etc.). The graphic files are in GIF format.

To purchase framed prints of cartoons or to license cartoons for use in periodicals, Web sites, or other media, please contact CARTOONBANK.COM. Tel: 800-897-TOON, or (914) 478-5527, Fax: (914) 478-5604, e-mail: toon@cartoonbank.com, Web: www.cartoonbank.com.